SWISS COOKIES

For Stella

our little cookie monster

Swiss Cookies: a home-baked cultural journey
ISBN: 978-3-03869-111-2
Also published in German as: *Schweizer Guetzli und andere Leckereien: eine Kulturreise durch die heimischen Backstuben*
ISBN: 978-3-03869-112-9

Layout and typesetting: Kimberly Smith
Additional Photos, pages 6, 8, 20, 23, 32, 35, 36, 39, 62, 84, 113, 134, 143, copyright Samuel Bucheli.
Photo, page 20 (top right), copyright Florian Bärtschiger.
Photo, page 36 (top left), copyright Kambly.
Photo, page 40, Staatsarchiv des Kantons Zürich

First edition: October 2021
Deposit copy in Switzerland: October 2021
Printed in the Czech Republic

Bergli is being supported by the Swiss Federal Office of Culture with a structural grant for the years 2021–2025.

www.bergli.ch

SWISS COOKIES

A home-baked cultural journey

by Andie Pilot

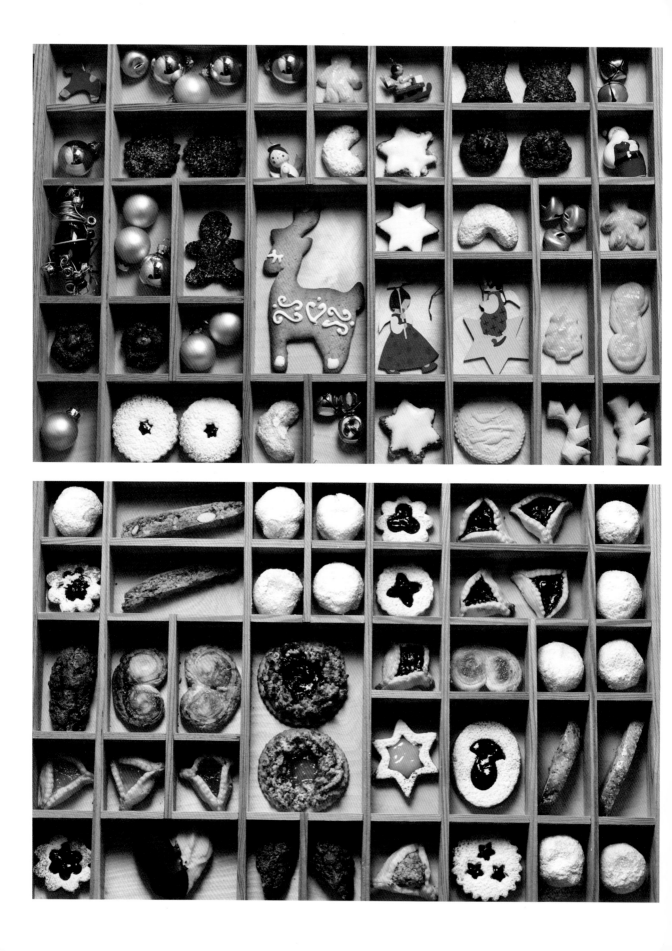

Table of Contents

My Cookie Romance

I feel uniquely positioned to write a book about cookies – I can smell them baking on most days, even if they aren't coming from our own oven.

That's because we live deep in the Emmental, Trubschachen, next to the Kambly cookie factory, which has been making cookies in our picturesque little village since 1910.

I live and breathe cookies.

My Swiss mother provided me with my first cookie memories, baking and eating Mailänderli and Brunsli in my hometown of Calgary. Her cookies were a favourite in the neighbourhood, and many of our friends still wax poetic about Mrs Pilot's Swiss Christmas Cookies. Becoming a pastry chef in 2009 expanded my cookie horizons, but it's still my mother's Guetzli that I aspire to.

I've been lucky to have not only her (and my grandmother's) cookie recipes, but also many entrusted by friends and family, including a whole shoebox full of old recipes from my husband Sam's grandmother. These beloved, no-fail recipes, a pile of old Swiss cookbooks and domestic school textbooks, plus invaluable time spent talking to home bakers and professionals, grandmothers and cookie-lovers, have helped me compile this book of the tastiest and most interesting cookies in Switzerland.

There are cookies you can find in shops and bakeries (like Leckerli and Lebkuchen), regional favourites (like Fuatscha Grassa from Graubünden and Pane dei Morti from Ticino), a selection of classic Swiss Christmas cookies, plus some modern cookies that use typically Swiss products like Ovomaltine, Birnenhonig (a syrup made from pears) and Magenträs (a sandalwood spice mix).

But there aren't only recipes. Take a peek behind the scenes at some of Switzerland's most notable cookie producers or see the painstaking process of making wooden cookie moulds. Swiss cookie history is compelling, and I'm certainly not the only person having a cookie love affair. Stay tuned for plenty of romance, as well as a prison sentence, drunks, a witch, a dead goose, and a buttery fortune teller.

Fire up your oven, get out your rolling pin, and soon you'll be living and breathing (Swiss) cookies too.

For more on my Swiss food adventures visit my website, helvetickitchen.com or on social media @helvetickitchen.

Andie Pilot

Trubschachen, Switzerland
September 2021

A Land of Cookie Lovers

There are home kitchens, warm and fragrant with lovingly-prepared Christmas cookies, regional bakeries using secret recipes to produce their cookie specialty, and big family-run factories, sourcing local ingredients to ensure a quality biscuit. In Switzerland there's a cookie for every taste.

Cookies are given as gifts, whether brought back from a trip (Bretzeli from the Emmental or Läckerli from Basel), or made at home and placed in beautiful holiday tins (extra Brunsli for me, please).

They are used to commemorate events, like the gingerbread Surseer Honiggans which depicts the strange tradition of beheading a dead goose, or preserve history, which is clear from the intricate designs on Zurich's honey-flavoured cookie, Tirggel.

Cookies show off the best of Switzerland because they involve

- high-quality ingredients: home bakers and large factories alike often use local ingredients, like butter from local cows and flour from local mills.

- hard work: every year I'm astounded by the numerous tins of Christmas cookies that my mother-in-law makes and distributes to family and friends, and this happens in households all over the country.

- patience: not only in the baking of cookies (which often requires long drying times) but some cookies themselves need to be appreciated slowly. The recommended eating method of many of the hard biscuits is to break them up, put a piece in your mouth and let it melt slowly.

- tradition: companies still use secret recipes from a century ago, families follow handwritten recipes from their mothers and grandmothers, and plenty of old baking tools are kept in pristine condition; whether it's the Kambly cookie factory using original iron cookie casts in an open fire, or pressing your dough into wooden cookie moulds that have been used in your family for generations.

Cookies are easy to transport, easy to share, and whether you make them ornate and elaborate, or plain and simple, they are bound to bring on the smiles.

You can have them at any time of day (Spitzbuben have jam, and that's a breakfast food, right?), and as much as we protest after eating dinner and dessert that we 'couldn't possibly' – when the coffee comes out, there's always space for a cookie.

Cookie Skills

Ingredients and Useful Tools

FLOUR: unless otherwise stated, most cookies in this book use regular white flour. It is good practice to sift the flour and other dry ingredients before combining with the wet ingredients.

BUTTER: different countries have different criteria for butter production – in Switzerland, butter has a minimum fat content of 82%. The most important thing to watch is the butter temperature: some recipes require the butter to be added cold, while others need it at room temperature (this will always be noted in the method).

EGGS: the recipes are calculated with standard Swiss eggs that have a weight of 53g+ (with shell) and the average weight for their parts is around 35 g white and 15 g yolk. If a recipe uses only the whites or yolks, I have included gram measurements for accuracy.

ICING SUGAR: also known as powdered or confectioner's sugar, always sift before adding to other ingredients to prevent lumps.

NUTS: ground nuts are readily available in Switzerland, however it's also possible to grind your own nuts using a mill or food processor. Add an extra boost of flavour by toasting nuts before adding them to a recipe. Just make sure you keep an eye on them, as they go from pale to burnt very quickly (I'm speaking from experience). Let them cool completely before adding them to the batter or dough.

CHOCOLATE: I typically use dark chocolate with 70% cocoa or higher. To melt chocolate for dipping, chop it finely and place it in a bowl over simmering water.

A SMALL OFFSET SPATULA: use this to transfer the cookies from the rolling surface to the baking sheet.

A SCRAPER: use this to portion dough or scrape up your dough scraps.

A ROLLING PIN: wooden, marble, with or without handles, use what feels comfortable to you.

COOKIE CUTTERS: metal cutters in lots of shape and sizes make for enjoyable cookie cutting. Don't forget the tiny ones for cutting the holes in your Spitzbuben tops.

WOODEN MOULDS: invaluable when making moulded cookies, Tirggel, or Zürcher Leckerli.

PIPING TIPS: the recipes in this book use 1 cm flat, round and star tips.

TEIGHÖLZLI: handy wooden (or plastic) sticks that sit alongside the dough while you're rolling – use them to ensure you get the thickness required. You can find these at larger supermarkets and department stores.

Cookie Skills

Making the dough or batter

CREAMING BUTTER AND SUGAR: Some recipes ask you to cream the butter and sugar, which means beating them together until pale and fluffy. This helps aerate the dough and makes lighter baked goods. It works best if your butter is at room temperature – the butter should give way when you press it with your finger. If eggs are added, they should also be at room temperature.

Although you can beat the butter and sugar by hand, it is much quicker and easier to use a stand mixer with paddle attachment or hand mixer with beaters.

RUBBING IN THE BUTTER: Some recipes ask for the butter to be rubbed into the dry ingredients, which creates flaky layers in the finished product. For this the butter (and other wet ingredients) should be cold.

Using your fingers, or a pastry blender, rub the butter into the flour mixture until you get small crumbs. Mix in any further wet ingredients quickly, taking care not to work the dough too much.

WHIPPING EGG WHITES: Although the following procedure isn't strictly necessary for all recipes with whipped whites, it's good practice for achieving light and airy end results, and it's essential when making baked goods like meringues.

Prepare your bowl by wiping it with an acid. Pour a drop of clear vinegar or lemon juice into the bowl, then use a paper towel to wipe the inside and then the whisk that you'll be using. This will remove any fat, which inhibits the whites from whipping fully, and helps form a stable foam.

Be careful when separating the yolks from the whites, as even a small bit of egg yolk in the whites will inhibit their foaming ability.

Start beating the whites slowly, then increase speed once they have turned foamy and white. Add sugar (if and when directed by the recipe), beating until you reach your desired stiffness – soft peaks are still a little droopy, but stiff peaks hold their form.

Cookie Skills

Forming and baking the cookies

ROLLING OUT DOUGH: For doughs that require chilling, here are three different techniques for rolling out:

1. Form the dough into a disc, chill, and then roll out using flour, sugar, or icing sugar. While rolling out, keep moving the dough on the table and making sure that it doesn't stick, adding more flour or sugar if necessary.

2. Form the dough into a disc, chill and then roll out between two sheets of parchment or plastic.

3. Place the freshly mixed dough (before chilling) on a piece of parchment or plastic, then place a piece of parchment or plastic over top and roll it out, then chill. This method avoids adding extra flour to the dough.

Depending on how long the dough has been in the fridge, it may be too hard to roll. You can leave it out on the counter for about ten minutes until it becomes more pliable.

To maintain an even thickness when you are rolling out the dough, try using Teighölzli. These handy wooden (or plastic) sticks sit alongside the dough while you're rolling, ensuring that you get the exact thickness required.

Once you've cut out the cookies, use an offset spatula to move them to the baking sheet.

LINING A BAKING SHEET: Most recipes call for parchment-lined baking sheets, though you can also use silicone baking mats, or lightly grease your baking sheet. I often use my parchment paper many times, wiping it off between batches. There are a couple of recipes (like Anisguetzli or Tirggel) that need an unlined, greased baking sheet, but that is mentioned in the recipe.

OVEN: For best results, rotate baking sheets halfway through baking. If you are baking all day, your oven will retain the heat better and get a little hotter as the day wears on – in later batches you can reduce the baking time slightly.

The baking times and temperatures in this book were tested using a convection oven. If you have a conventional oven, you may have to raise the temperature by about 20° C. I find that ovens bake differently and that it's most important to look at the cookies themselves. I generally bake the cookies one tray at a time, in the middle of the oven, unless otherwise specified.

Cookie Skills

The finished product

STORING COOKIES: Cool cookies completely before placing them in airtight containers. Metal tins tend to keep firm cookies crisp, and plastic is better to keep soft cookies soft.

It's nice to assemble tins with multiple varieties of cookies for giving as gifts, but when storing at home, keep each type of cookie in a separate container, not together.

If you have sticky, decorated, or delicate cookies, place them between layers of parchment or wax paper.

FREEZING COOKIES: Most of the cookies in this book can be frozen either before or after baking.

Butter doughs can be frozen in discs and thawed overnight in the fridge, then rolled and cut out as usual.

You can freeze logs of cookie dough – let thaw on the counter for about 20 minutes, then cut out and bake (use a serrated knife and take care when cutting).

You can freeze already cut-out cookies directly on parchment-lined baking sheets and bake them from frozen.

Already baked cookies can also be frozen in airtight plastic containers. They keep for about three months in the freezer.

MAKE NOTES: Get out your pencils and sticky notes and fill this cookbook with your own baking notes. It's always hard to remember what the Christmas cookies were like last year – maybe you added an extra teaspoon of ginger somewhere that your family went wild for – so be sure to make a quick note in your book so you'll know for next year.

Seven Historic Swiss Cookies

The following seven cookies: Basler Leckerli, Zürcher Leckerli, Berner Haselnusslebkuchen, Biberli, Bretzeli, Tirggel, and Willisauer Ringli, aren't necessarily Switzerland's oldest, though many are quite old. Most of them started out in home kitchens and eventually became so beloved in their regions that they began to be mass produced. Today they can all be bought commercially (though some more easily than others) and in a few cases the factories that make them are some of Switzerland's largest cookie producers.

I've been through scores of old recipe books and spoken to producers to gather tips for home bakers. I've scaled down the quantities and reduced the resting and chilling times as much as possible while still maintaining the essence of the cookies.

I hope they bring you fond memories of cookies you remember, or introduce you to a new cookie to love.

Jakob's Basler— Leckerly

ÄLTESTE BISCUIT MANUFAKTUR 1753

Jakob's Basler Leckerly

Switzerland's oldest cookie company

Throw open a Baedeker travel guide from 1844 and you'll see the advice to visit Steiger'schen's (today Jakob's) Basler Leckerly, to taste the famous Basel treat from a company that had already existed for about a century.

'Leckerli could have been eaten by every US president, were he so inclined,' says Andreas Kuster who, with his wife Charlotte, are the current owners of the company, today one of Switzerland's thirty oldest.

Basel born and bred, Andreas remembers the Leckerli of his childhood. When it was time to make the family's Christmas batch, his mother would call for him, his father and brother, and task them with kneading the dough – muscle was required for Leckerli baking. It's a taste from childhood, and one that he is now proud to offer to the public.

The current selection of Leckerli in the shop is a trip through time, baked according to recipes from each century. Their 1700s version is heavy on honey and has large pieces of almonds mixed in. The 1800s are focused on fruit, with candied peel balancing the traditional honey flavour. And for a 1900s twist, they dip their Leckerli in chocolate.

Today, a kilogram of Leckerli would set you back about 30 CHF but, according to Andreas, when the shop opened in 1753 the price per kilo would have been about 500 CHF. That's due to the expensive ingredients contained within.

The treat became popular in the city in the 1700s. It was initially baked at home, and later became a source of income for all kinds of households, especially those of widows. However, this displeased the baker's guild, who wanted to standardise production and control who was allowed to sell the treat, likely driving up the price. Fortunately it was declared an unprotected good in 1716 and again in 1720, much to the chagrin of the guild.

As Andreas told me 'it was the community that evolved the cookie.' Every family passed around their own tips and tricks, and from there the Leckerli evolved into the symbol of Basel that it is today.

Tip

If you can hire piano movers to help you knead the dough, do so...The dough can be quite sticky, so if you need to roll it out use plenty of flour and simply brush it off afterwards. You don't have to bother making a complicated cooked sugar icing – a simple icing sugar glaze will do (I've included a variant in my recipe as well).

Leckerly, Läckerli, Leckerli, Läggerli

Why so many names for a single baked good?

The Leckerli known in Basel today can be traced back to the 1300s when the Lebkuchen trade developed in Europe, particularly in monasteries. In fact, many of the oldest books list the specialty as Lebkuchen, with its first appearance as Leckerlÿ in a 1741 cookbook by Anna Magdalena Falkeysen, whose handwritten recipe can still be viewed in the Basel city archive.

The word itself most likely comes from the German verb *lecken* or *schlecken*, to lick. Indeed *Schleckzeug*, German for something to lick, is another name for a sweet. And to complicate matters there weren't only Leckerli from Basel, but other parts of the country had their own Leckerli, like the ones from Zurich that are similar to marzipan.

As for the spelling, like many dialect words this varied over time. For example, the 'y' in Jakob's Basler Leckerly was simply a way to make their product more appealing to English tourists.

The many names of Leckerli, as well as their varying ingredients, were compiled by Albert Spycher, the great Swiss food historian, is his book *Leckerli aus Basel* (a cultural history of the specialty, published in 1991). He presents a spectacular chart of every old Leckerli recipe from the 18th and 19th century, both from private families and from bakeries.

His chart lists the differing quantities of ingredients, as well as tips, like the suggestion to use very old honey (one baker insists it should be aged at least six years), or to warm the flour in the oven before adding it to the honey, or to first set the kirsch aflame.

Anna von der Mühle's recipe from 1847 is one of the many that gives us a glimpse of how Leckerli might have been produced, at home, en masse.

'Two hands to hold the bowl, two hands to mix vigorously, because you need to work quickly and nimbly, as the dough cools quickly and becomes tough and stiff...'

Anna Maria Fäsch's recipe from 1796, echoes the sentiment. She adds all the ingredients to the bubbling honey and suggests mixing *'bis man nimmer kann'* – until you can't mix anymore.

Basler Leckerli

Unlike the old recipes, this one doesn't require a partner (or an army) for mixing. I've scaled it down, and strong biceps or a stand mixer will do, but be sure to work the dough while it's still warm.

INGREDIENTS

makes 30

300 g flour
1 tsp baking powder
200 g honey
120 g sugar
120 g ground almonds
60 g candied peel (lemon and orange), minced
the zest of half a lemon
1 tsp cinnamon
pinch each cloves and nutmeg
50 ml kirsch

Cooked sugar glaze
20 ml water
40 g sugar

Easy glaze
75 g icing sugar
2 tbsp milk

METHOD

Preheat oven to 200° C.

Sift the flour and baking powder into a large bowl. Set aside.

In a medium pot, warm the honey over medium heat. Add the sugar and stir until dissolved. Remove from the heat and stir in the almonds, candied peel, zest and spices. Stir in the kirsch.

Pour the honey mixture into the flour mixture while stirring continuously. Mix well.

Place the dough directly on a piece of floured parchment paper. Using plenty of flour, roll out to a large rectangle 30 x 24 cm and 1 cm thick. Slide the paper on to a baking sheet.

Bake for about 12-15 min, or until the top is golden. Glaze immediately with either the cooked sugar glaze or the easy glaze. Let cool and slice into 6 x 4 cm rectangles.

Cooked sugar glaze
In a small pot over high heat, cook together the water and sugar until syrupy and the temperature reaches 108° C, then immediately brush over the still warm Leckerli.

Easy glaze
Whisk together and brush over the still warm Leckerli.

Zürcher Leckerli

These beautiful sweets from Zurich are essentially a flavoured marzipan, pressed into wooden forms. Quite unlike other, gingerbready Leckerli found in Switzerland (especially Basel) these detailed beauties can be coloured and flavoured with a range of different nuts and spices, like green pistachios, dark chocolate, or pink sandalwood.

Although it's not clear exactly when Zurich's variation of the Leckerli took shape, recipes for it started appearing in 1912. Like Tirggel, another of Zurich's historic sweets, it was also popular with guilds, who could stamp it with their insignia. Both were holiday favourites, given as gifts and used as decoration.

INGREDIENTS

makes 30

200 g blanched, ground almonds
180 g icing sugar
1 egg white (35 g)
a few drops bitter almond or almond extract

METHOD

Pulse together the nuts and icing sugar in a food processor or grinder until very fine. Remove to a bowl. Add the egg white and almond extract, then stir until you can form a dough.

Using icing sugar, roll out dough to about 0.5 cm thick. Dust with more icing sugar and press with wooden forms to create designs on the surface. With a cutter or knife, cut out 4x6 cm individual pieces and gently brush off excess icing sugar. Place on parchment-lined baking sheets. If possible, let dry for a few hours, or overnight (this helps preserve the design).

When you are ready to bake

Preheat oven to 160° C, top heat. Bake for about 6-8 minutes or until they look dry, but have gained no colour. If desired, you can glaze the Leckerli: mix 30 g icing sugar with about 1 tbsp water and brush over while still warm.

Variations

Pistachio: replace half the ground almonds with pistachios, and grind this together with the icing sugar and almonds in the food processor. Omit the almond extract.

Sandalwood: replace 30 g icing sugar with 30 g Magenträs (see page 99), or 10 g icing sugar with 10 g sandalwood powder. Omit almond extract.

Chocolate: Instead of egg white, add 35 g melted dark chocolate.

Berner
Haselnusslebkuchen

In the 19th century, Bern's Haselnusslebkuchen (called Berner Leckerli at the time) was a luxury and typically given as a gift, especially at Christmas. Today, it is available year round from plenty of bakeries in the city and further afield in the canton.

It typically features Bern's symbolic bear in some form, either moulded into the cookie or piped on in icing. Another option would be to do as some of the old cookbooks suggest and forgo the bear entirely, making a simple pattern with the tongs of a fork.

INGREDIENTS

makes 16 large or 32 small

240 g icing sugar
2 egg whites (70 g)
80 g honey
200 g ground hazelnuts, toasted
150 g ground almonds, toasted
80 g candied peel, chopped finely
1 tsp cinnamon

METHOD

In a large bowl, whisk together the icing sugar and egg white. Warm the honey over low heat and once it has liquefied, whisk into the egg mixture. Add the rest of the ingredients and mix until combined.

The dough should be quite sticky. Gather it into a disc, wrap and chill in the fridge for a couple of hours until it feels firm to the touch. Using icing sugar, roll out the dough to about 0.7 cm thick. If you are using wooden forms, dust them with icing sugar, then press into the dough to create designs on the surface. With a cutter or knife, cut out individual pieces and gently brush off excess icing sugar. Otherwise, cut out rectangles about 6x10 cm for large and 6x5 cm for small cookies. If you are icing bears on top you can leave them plain, otherwise you can use a fork to make a simple design on the dough. Place on a parchment-lined baking sheet.

At this stage you can let the cookies rest at room temperature for a couple of hours or overnight – this produces a nice crust, and helps the modelled cookies keep their shape when baked – or you can bake them right away.

When you are ready to bake

Preheat the oven to 200° C. Bake for about 10 minutes, or until the bottoms are just starting to brown.

If you like, ice a bear on the surface...and don't forget its tongue (recipe for royal icing on page 136).

Biberli

In countless mountain restaurants, gondola stations and lakeside kiosks you'll find Bärli-Biber, a small, marzipan-stuffed gingerbread with an Appenzeller scene on the package. These treats, also known as Biberli and made by the Appenzeller company Bischofsberger, are a smaller version of the canton's large gingerbread Biber.

Today the Biberli are beloved snacks, pulled out of backpacks in the middle of a hike, or from beach bags beside the lake.

My recipe is a simplified version of the treat – in Eastern Swiss bakeries the dough is often left to ripen overnight, or even as long as two weeks, before being filled and baked. It's sometimes moulded, but here you can simply leave it plain or ice something pretty on top.

INGREDIENTS

makes 15

100 g honey
100 g sugar
150 ml milk
1 egg yolk (15 g)
325 g light whole wheat flour
10 g baking powder
10 g Lebkuchen spice mix
1/2 tsp salt

Assembly
1 recipe marzipan (see page 136)
Milk or cream

TIP
In Switzerland the flour to use is *Ruchmehl / farine bise / farina bigia*. If desired, decorate with royal icing, recipe on page 136. Don't have Lebkuchen spice mix? You can make your own – recipe on page 136.

METHOD

In a small pot over low heat warm the honey. Once it has liquified, whisk in the sugar and remove from the heat.

In a separate bowl, whisk together the milk and egg yolk, then whisk in the honey mixture.

In a large bowl, whisk together the flour, baking powder, Lebkuchen spice, and salt. Stir in the honey mixture until you get a soft dough.

Using flour, roll out dough to 0.5 cm thick and cut out 30 rounds (8 cm diameter). Sandwich a thick disc of marzipan between two dough rounds and press the edges together.

Place on parchment-lined baking sheets, brush with a little milk or cream, then bake in the top part of the oven for about 10-12 minutes, or until the bottoms are golden.

Bretzeli / Bricelets

Beautiful cookies, hot off the presses

Bretzeli, or Bricelets as they are known in French, are a popular cookie in many parts of Switzerland, especially Bern and Fribourg. A dough or batter is placed in a hot press, which indents a design on the cookie. Then they are either rolled up, folded, or left flat.

Today, many families treasure their *fer à bricelets / Brezeleisen*, an electric device that looks a bit like a waffle iron with pretty designs, sometimes including the Swiss flag. Although there are some affordable new models available, the vintage presses from the Swiss firm Jura (of coffee machine fame) are a hot commodity and regularly go for over 300 CHF on the second-hand market.

Original *fer à bricelets / Brezeleisen*, as the name suggests, were made from *fer* or *Eisen,* iron. They had long handles, were elaborately decorated with coats of arms, religious or patriotic themes, and would have been heated over an open fire.

Pressed cookies have been made in Europe since the 1200s, likely originating from the making of the host, the wafer consumed in Catholic mass, which was also originally created by a hot iron press.

In Fribourg the Bricelets are an important part of the Bénichon festival, a harvest fair held in autumn that features many of the canton's most delicious culinary specialties. The family of my Fribourgeois friend Johanna makes yet another variation, the Seisler Brätzele, which eschews the normal Bretzeli shapes in favour of a double crossing loop. Her aunt swears by slightly soured cream to give it that something special, and makes both sweet and savoury versions.

Whatever kind you make, it's a labour of love, and one that often involves a crew of helpers to assist with the rolling or cutting of cookies, hot off the presses.

Bretzeli

When I arrived at my husband's childhood home, my mother-in-law Josy already had all the Bretzeli making paraphernalia arranged on her kitchen table: her black and white handwritten notebook of recipes, an assortment of wooden spoons, two bottles of 'the good *Most*' (the apple cider from Mosterei Möhl) and of course her beautiful beige Jura *Brezeleisen*. I was there to be initiated into the family's Bretzeli making.

The no-fail recipe for rolled-up Bretzeli comes from Josy's mother-in-law, Marie, who attended domestic school, then married and raised her nine children on a farm in canton Lucerne. Her old recipe books provide insight into Swiss farm life at the time and her Bretzeli were always a hit.

The procedure might vary depending on the type of Bretzeli press you have, so be sure to read the manufacturer's instructions for tips on your machine.

INGREDIENTS

makes 35

a little oil for greasing
250 g flour
250 g sugar
250 ml Saurer Most or white wine
250 ml whipping cream
1 tbsp kirsch

TIP
Saurer Most, not so sweet apple cider, can be alcoholic or not, and is available all over Switzerland.

METHOD

In a large bowl, whisk together all the ingredients.

Make sure the press is hot, lightly brush with a little oil, spoon the batter into the middle (not too much, it will spread) then close the lid and wait about 30 seconds. Open and check – once it is golden and just starting to turn brown, roll it up around the back of a wooden spoon. Peel it off with help from a plastic or wooden scraper (like a raclette scraper), or your fingernails if you're feeling brave.

When it is cool enough to touch, slide off with your hand and let cool on a rack.

It may take you a couple of times to get a feel for how much batter to use and when and how to roll.

The exact number of Bretzeli is a bit variable and depends on exactly how much batter you use and how much (delicious) waste you produce in your initial attempts at using the press. Josy's Bretzeli are always very thin and delicate, while my husband Sam's tend to be a bit thicker and crunchier and have a slightly lower yield.

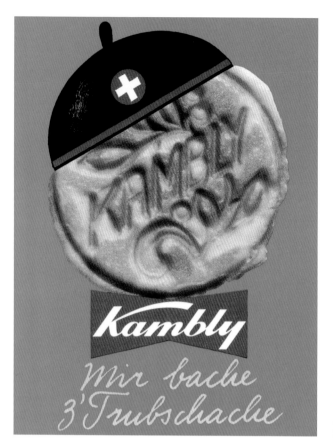

Mir bache
3'Trubschache

The Kambly Cookie Factory

Love from the Emmental Valley

If anyone knows cookies, it's Ursula Kambly, who works as vice president of the board of directors, and in strategic development at the Kambly cookie factory, the company founded by her husband's grandfather. But, like most Swiss people, her earliest memories of cookies are Christmas baking.

'The classics,' she says with a smile, counting them off on her fingers 'Mailänderli, Brunsli, Zimtsterne, Spitzbuben.'

Her favourite? The elegant Vanille Kipferl.

Ursula Kambly's grandmother also made Bretzeli for the family, an item so treasured that her mother would pack them in tins and hide them away. One year, like the squirrels, she forgot where she hid the tin and it was only discovered by chance nearly a year later. To the great joy of her family, they were in almost perfect condition and quickly enjoyed.

Bretzeli are Kambly's most beloved product, and one that they have baked with an unchanged recipe since the beginning, 111 years ago. Oscar R. Kambly followed his sweetheart, a girl from the Emmental, back to her village of Trubschachen, and there he started one of Switzerland's best and most successful cookie companies.

The secret to Kambly's success lies in a total commitment to the quality of the product they make. Their ingredients come from the rolling hills around the factory – flour from the local mill and butter from local cows. Every day the factory produces three tonnes of Bretzeli, more than enough to feed each resident of Zurich, Geneva and Lucerne.

For Ursula Kambly, the most important part of home cookie baking is joy. Being excited about the cookies you're making and sharing this delight with others. This extends to children in the kitchen, joyfully smushing the dough and sneaking tastes, both important parts of the process.

The Haldemann Mill

Flour for a famous cookie

'Kambly Bretzeli,' replied Beat Haldemann, when I asked him his favourite cookie.

And why not, that's his flour inside.

The Haldemann mill in Trubschachen has been providing flour to the Kambly cookie factory for over a century. With no actual contract in place, it was a shake of hands between the elder Haldemann and Kambly in 1910 that sealed the deal, one that still exists today.

The mill itself has been in operation since 1860, and Beat and his wife Evelyn are already its fifth generation of family owners. On the day I visited, Beat showed me the three floors of the mill. The grain is brought to the top and through a complicated system of tubes is transported through the grinding machines until the desired fineness is reached.

And it's loud.

There's the sound of the machines, plus all of the moving parts, spinning, whooshing, grinding, but it doesn't bother Beat, who moves deftly around, quickly dipping his hand in different machines to show me the different stages of the grinding process.

A wheat kernel is made up of three parts – the endosperm (the part used for making white flour), and the bran (its outer shell) and germ (the wheat seed), which are used for whole wheat flours. It's the miller's job to separate the parts of a wheat (or spelt or rye) kernel and grind them down – in the Haldemann mill this is still done using beautiful burgundy machines that were manufactured in Zurich in 1948. The freshly milled white flour is soft, light and fluffy, and I feel fortunate to be able to use it in my own kitchen.

Along with providing Kambly with their flour, the Haldemann mill also produces flours from wheat and UrDinkel (pure spelt) for the general public.The byproducts from the flour production are then used to make animal feed.

For cookie baking, the miller himself recommends the mill's *Weissmehl* (white flour). You can buy Haldemann flour directly from the mill, or in many local shops and supermarkets in the region.

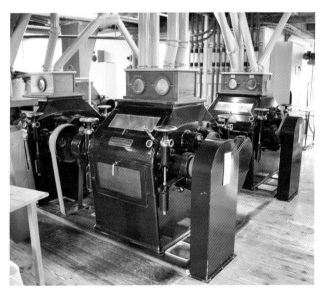

Uff den grossen und mercklichen lümbden, der jn Margreth bucherin des stuks von
oberwil In der herschaft andelfingen gelegen, und lange jar gewesen ist,
haben ain herren sy In jr fangenschafft bringen, och dem nach umb jr
blümdigung fragen lassen, und als aber sy keinerley vsehen wolt, ward
jr offt befolch min herren zügesagt, sy umb keinerley sach zu töden, dz sy nun
die warheit sagte, damit und doch nun hien desshalb, dero bericht wurden, Uff
das hat sy dis nachgeschriben verjehen, war sin.

Item das by eym halben jar, she gebe sy einem brunen tund wee rudy stuks
ein krut zu essen, darab es stürbe, Och hab sy vor jarn jn gross gschwellent gmacht
Sy hab och rudin stukin ein wiß roß vderzt

Item In disem jar hab sy etlich krut, und brunen ku und einem wissen roß
och zu essen geben, die och stürbind, die beide weren heiny stuks,
Sy hab och heiny stuks trochter zu essend geben, daran sy sarben müsse und
och stürbe

Item hab sy heiny stuks trochter einer zu essen geben ein kruchly, und dathe
thon, dz sy stürbe

Item hausen stukin heiny stuks sun, hab sy bulver von gifft jn win zu
trinken geben, dz er stürbe

Item rudin huber von tütwil, hab sy an sin hand erlempt, und jn dem nach
wider gsund gemacht, mit unrecht hebel

Item burgin müller hab sy och erlembdt, und jm jn ein trüggely gifft zu
essen geben, dz er stürbe

Item klasen stukin hab sy och ein wiß roß vderzt

Sy hab och den lüt dick von jren kügen milch genomen, also dz sy ein axe
In ein first sul schlüge, und dem nach die milch heruß liesse, ec.

Item ein genant hans jerg von Unfra, hab sy und jr schwöster, dz mit dem
krut ob sy den rindt zu essen geben hab, gelert

Dis hat sy
widerrüfft
So hab sy jr trochter die eltern dz och gelert und wz sy kön, dz künd och
jr schwöster und jr trochter

Item Sy hab sich dem tüfel ergeben, der redte och gegen jr, Sy solt jr sachen
machen wie sy welt, Er hab och vil jar mit jr züthschafft gehept In
bülschaft wis, und kemen alweg zusammen zu tägeilen, by dem
bildstöckly an der wegscheide, da keme er zu jr, als ein grosser swartz
hund, etliche sy och nie gebicht, und darüber dz heilig sacrament
empfange het.

Double Double Tirggel Trouble

Gift from a witch

The recorded history of so many Swiss cookies is a romantic one – bakers giving recipes to their sweethearts or sending messages in dough. Tirggel, Zurich's crispy honey biscuit, also served to pass love letters, which were pressed into the dough using intricate wooden forms.

However, one of the earliest records of Tirggel had nothing to do with lovers, but a woman named Margreth Bucher, who was accused of being a witch.

The case against her was heard by the Zurich state court on May 2, 1487, and the accusations included the paralysis or death of numerous cattle and people, turning milk into blue flame, and copulation with the devil. The direct mention of Tirggel came in this line:

'She is said to also have disabled Bürgi Müller and given him poisoned Tirggel, so he would die.'

The court promised her that they would let her live if she confessed everything, which she did. Her sentence? Being walled up alive.

'[that they] shall let said Margreth be walled up alive such that neither sun nor moon would ever shine on her again [...]'

You can still find the court transcript for this (and the nearly 80 additional witch trials that occurred in Zurich up until 1701) in Zurich's cantonal archive. The historian and former director Otto Sigg published a transcription of all the trials in 2012, which is available online, in German.

The Suter Tirggel Factory

Survival of the biscuits

With her baskets of allotted cookies (plus a secret stash stuffed under her skirts), Wilhelmine Suter boarded the boat in Wädenswil, on the lake of Zurich. The Suters had made Tirggel, the beloved honey biscuits popular in the city, for years, but it was only in 1840 when they were actually granted permission to sell them, as distribution of baked goods was strictly controlled. However, with her husband newly allergic to flour and unable to deliver, or make, the cookies, it was up to Wilhelmine to take the daily trip to sell to the bakeries of Zurich.

Tirggel production wasn't easy work. Suter's factory had no electricity, so all the production was done by hand – including baking the cookies over wood fires. The dough was sticky and made in huge batches, requiring brute strength to knead it, roll it out, and cut it. But somehow they managed.

At the height of the Industrial Revolution the factory was finally electrified, and the family bought a large cookie press from England that is still fully-functional and used today.

In the first half of the twentieth century, the company was passed on to the next generation, the charismatic Willy Suter. Under his management they survived while so many others crumbled under the weight of falling markets and war.

During the Second World War Suter himself went to Bern to request more flour rations and, when he was denied, he forged the permits himself, eventually landing in jail. Released at the end of the war, he went back to cookie baking, and ran the business until 1972, when it was bought by Peter Seibold, who headed it until 2008, when it was sold to Carlo Magnano, the current owner.

Carlo Magnano, who was raised nearby and remembers eating Tirggel for the first time as a child at his aunt's house, honours the tradition of the company. He is delighted when his elderly customers reminisce about the Tirggel of their childhood.

'Neighbourhood kids were always treated to free Tirggel if they knocked on the factory door – they still are today,' he says with a grin.

The recipe hasn't changed much in a century and now, as then, honey is the star of the show. These are not cookies to eat quickly, instead break one into pieces and let the honey flavour unfold on the tongue. It's the same flavour you smell as soon as you walk into Suter's Tirggel factory in Schönenberg today, and one that Carlo Magnano intends to keep.

Tirggel

Tirggel was a favourite treat of guilds, especially as it was popular to have the emblem of the guild pressed into the cookie. After long meetings and merrymaking, the guild members would tipsily sway home with the honey-flavoured cookie in hand (penance for their wives) amongst catcalls echoing in the street 'he's got a Tirggel!', which became a synonym for being drunk.

Today, Tirggel is available throughout the year, but especially enjoyed at Christmas time. Bakeries use historic wooden forms to make beautiful patterns on the cookies, and you can even buy Schnapps flavoured with the famous Zurich treat.

INGREDIENTS

yield depends on the size
of the forms

220 g honey
50 g icing sugar
1 tsp cinnamon
1 tsp kirsch
280 g flour

METHOD

In a pot over low heat, warm the honey until it liquefies, then whisk in the sugar. Once it has dissolved, remove from heat. Stir in the cinnamon and kirsch, then gently sift in the flour and mix in well. Wrap and let rest for a couple of hours at room temperature.

Using flour, roll out the dough to about 0.3-0.5 cm thick. Dust with more flour and press with wooden forms to create designs on the surface. Using a cutter or knife, cut out individual pieces and brush off any excess flour. Place on a lightly greased baking sheets (do not use parchment paper, as this might burn).

To best preserve the design, let dry for a few hours, or overnight.

When you are ready to bake

Preheat oven to 230° C, top heat.

Bake in the top part of the oven, checking after a minute or so and removing them once the top is brown and the underside is still pale. I usually stand next to the oven and keep the oven door slightly open to watch the browning.

Willisauer Ringli

From the castle to the masses

Another of Switzerland's cookie love stories began in a castle in canton Lucerne and it's one that has been passed down through the decades. In 1946, Willi Meyer told the tale at the Wiggertal *Heimattag* (a celebration of traditions in the Wiggertal, the region around Willisau) and it was later published in the organization's annual magazine, the *Heimatkunde*.

It begins in Schloss Heidegg, a castle built in 1185 by a knight of the same name, and today famous for its vineyards and beautiful rose garden. Throughout the centuries it was owned by different wealthy families, and it was Elisabeth Pfyffer and her husband who lived there in the mid-1800s. During that time, Martha Peyer, the daughter of Elisabeth's cousin, came to work at the castle as a young cook.

Martha also had a cousin, Anna, who was married to a baker in town, Heinrich Maurer. As a young man, Heinrich decided not to take over his father's farm and instead did his baking apprenticeship, landing in the small town of Willisau. Although he left and worked in other parts of the country, he always found himself returning to Willisau and eventually married Anna, his local sweetheart.

When Anna's father died in 1846, Heinrich bought their family's home on the main street and turned it into a bakery. Anna gave birth to three children, though sadly only one survived, their son, Robert. Anna herself died in 1857.

Now back to the castle. The year after Anna's death Martha left Schloss Heidegg and came to Willisau...to marry the baker.

Martha brought her long experience as a cook, as well as one particular recipe – a hard, citrus-flavoured cookie in the shape of a ring. Heinrich took her recipe, tweaked it so it could be mass produced, and named it after his adopted town, Willisauer Ringli. The cookie became so popular that other bakers began to copy it. In response, Heinrich's son Robert had the following painted on the side of the house, which you can still see on the building today:

'Here, according to tradition, Willisauer rings are made and sold. It is known throughout the country that this is where they come from.'

Robert didn't stray far from home. In 1877 he married a neighbour, Kunigunde Brun, and Heinrich took the young woman into his confidence (rather than his son, who had, in the meantime, become a politician). The experienced baker taught her how to make his famous Ringli. She kept the recipe secret and continued baking the specialty when her father-in-law died in 1882 and up until her husband's death in 1922. Soon after she sold the recipe and bakery to Moritz Amrein, whose descendants still bake the cookie today.

Today Café Amrein keeps the exact Ringli recipe under wraps, but there is a wonderful old video from the Swiss Broadcasting Corporation (SRG SSR) of bakers taking trays of rings to Willisau's central square before baking. There they were rinsed under the town fountain, which helped create an extra hard and shiny biscuit. Today they just get a spritz of water before entering the oven.

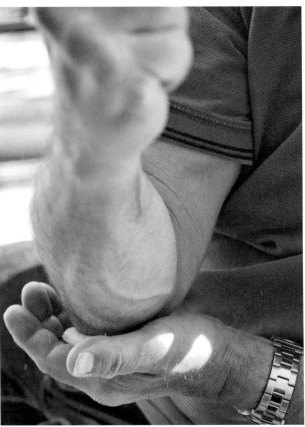

Tooth breakers

How to eat Willisauer Ringli

Willisauer Ringli remain a popular treat all over Switzerland...to the great pleasure of dentists. There are numerous jokes and anecdotes about people damaging their teeth on the very hard biscuits.

People in the know suggest breaking them up beforehand, and here's how to do it:

1. Place the cookie in the palm of your hand.
2. Press your opposite elbow into the hole in the cookie.
3. It should break into three or four pieces.
4. One by one, let the pieces dissolve on your tongue.

On the facing page you can see one in the large, capable hands of my father-in-law, Robert, who grew up not too far from Willisau and spent his working life as a large animal vet.

Willisauer Ringli

This recipe comes from my husband's grandmother, Marie. The rings aren't quite as dark and dense as the ones you find in Willisau (and they're missing the white spots, though you can add these by rolling the dough with pearl sugar), but they are sufficiently hard and have the characteristic citrus flavour.

INGREDIENTS

makes 40

100 ml water
250 g sugar
zest of one lemon
zest of one orange
250 g flour

METHOD

Preheat oven to 160° C.

Measure the water and sugar into a small pot. Place over high heat and, without stirring, let cook.

Once it has started boiling, start checking the temperature and when it reaches 108° C, take it off the heat. (In the original recipe, the instructions say to bring the sugar to a boil and let it boil for three minutes – if you don't have a thermometer you can use this method).

Add the zest and let the syrup cool until it is no longer hot to the touch, but still warm. Sift in the flour and stir to make a smooth dough.

Using flour, roll out the dough to 0.3–0.5 cm thick. Cut rounds (5 cm in diameter) and place on parchment-lined baking sheets, then cut out the centres.

Spritz or brush the rings lightly with water, then bake for about 10–12 minutes or until the bottoms are lightly golden.

n Vanillezucker oder 100 gr ... ... Zubereitung

Zubereitung: Die Creme wird wie eine Vanillecreme zubere...
nur gibt man, wenn sie dick geworden ist ...
50 gr Butter dazu.

Willisauerringli.

Zutaten: 3 dl Wasser, 500 gr Zucker, 500 gr Mehl, Schale ...
1-2 Zitronen.

Zubereitung: Das Wasser wird mit dem Zucker ca. 3 M...
gekocht, Zitronenrinde beigegeben u. den ...
erkalten gelassen. Er soll ziemlich dick se...
Das Mehl wird allmählich dazugegeben. Es sol...

Zutaten: 5

Zubereitung

The Surseer Honiggans

Cookies as commemoration

Pressed into the surface of soft gingerbread is the image of a pained looking goose with a sword at its neck.

This is the Surseer Honiggans ('honey goose').

Moulded cookies have been around for centuries, and there are plenty of baked goods commemorating local culture, but this sad goose and the tradition that spawned it is one of the strangest that still exists in Switzerland today.

The goose is the main feature of the Gansabhauet, an event that takes place every year on St Martin's Day, November 11, in Sursee, a small city in canton Lucerne.

At three in the afternoon, officiants (in black and yellow robes) and musicians (in red and white robes) parade into the main square, carrying two dead geese. The first bird is suspended from a wire that runs across the stage.

The participants (locals who have signed up and are chosen by lottery) are dressed in a red robe, blindfolded, masked with a giant golden sun head, and given a glass of wine. With two drummers leading the way, they are brought to the stage, spun around, handed their sword, and then must carefully feel around until they locate the goose. They get one chance to swipe and sever the goose's neck, and it can take anywhere from three to twenty hits before the goose falls and the participant who dealt the final blow can take their winnings home for dinner.

Historically, similar contests were held throughout Europe with varied fowl, a valuable prize. Participation in such a contest was also thought to be an incentive to encourage farmers to come to the city to pay their taxes.

Today the competition is (unsurprisingly) heavily criticised by animal activists for its barbaric nature, though many of the citizens of the town defend the old custom and enjoy eating their own geese, in cookie form.

Classic Swiss Cookies

Whether they come from Grosi's (grandma's) kitchen or your local bakery, you eat them year round, or only on special occasions, you'll find some of Switzerland's most beloved cookies on the following pages. From all regions of the country you'll find cookies that are dark, dense, chocolatey, crispy, crunchy, light, airy, nutty, buttery – something to suit every taste.

The *Gspüri*

Many old recipes talk about the *Gspüri*, the feeling for the dough. It's the confidence of knowing exactly how the dough should look and feel (and smell and taste). If you've baked a recipe enough times to get a real feeling for exactly how it should be, and you can get the same results every time you bake it, then you have the *Gspüri*.

There are so many variables in baking, especially cookies. Over and over again as I spoke to bakers – whether professionals or grandmothers – they all said the same thing: take your time.

The time you take to make your cookies – with someone, for someone – is an expression of your love for them.

Amaretti

Amaretti, the almond-and-egg-white biscuits popular throughout Italy, are also a popular cookie in Ticino. In Italy, their variations are typically hard and crunchy or soft and tender, but the Ticino version is crunchy on the outside with a soft middle.

Although plain versions are perfectly nice, for me the best amaretti are filled with kirsch (or grappa) cream and dipped in chocolate. My variation, meant to honour Ticino's local produce, is filled with chestnut purée.

INGREDIENTS

makes 16

250 g blanched, ground almonds
80 g sugar
2 egg whites (70 g)
1 tsp vanilla paste or extract
3 drops bitter almond or almond extract
icing sugar

Kirsch cream filling
60 g butter
40 g icing sugar
1 tbsp kirsch

Chestnut filling
100 g chestnut paste
1 tbsp kirsch

Assembly
150 g dark chocolate, melted

METHOD

In a food processor, grind the almonds and sugar until fine. Using an electric mixer with a whisk attachment, whisk the egg whites until stiff, then fold in the almonds and flavouring.

With wet hands, form the dough into 16 domes (5-6 cm in diameter). While you are forming the domes, use a finger or the back of a wooden spoon to make a hollow space in the bottom where the filling will go.

Place on a parchment-lined baking sheet and slightly flatten the tops with the palm of your hand. If desired, let dry for a few hours, or overnight (this helps maintain their shape).

When you are ready to bake

Preheat oven to 160° C.

Dust with icing sugar and bake for about 12-15 minutes, or until the bottoms are slightly golden. Let cool completely.

Assembly

Beat together the ingredients for either the kirsch cream or the chestnut filling, then pipe or spoon into the cookie.

Chill the cookies until the filling is firm (about an hour in the fridge, or 15 minutes in the freezer), then dip in melted chocolate.

Baisers XOXO

Baisers, French for kisses, is another name for meringues. These crisp, light confections made from whipped egg whites and sugar come in all shapes, sizes and flavours.

Sometimes the meringue that you get at a bakery is a chocolate one, piped in the shape of the letter 'S'. That's the kind I'm including here, though I thought my kisses might look better as Xs and Os (and they can double for a quick game of tic-tac-toe).

INGREDIENTS

makes 24

60 g chocolate, chopped
1/2 tsp salt
3 egg whites (105 g)
180 g sugar

METHOD

Preheat the oven to 150° C.

First melt the chocolate – either in a bowl over a pot of simmering water or in the microwave. Let cool while you prepare the meringue.

Using an electric mixer with a whisk attachment, start whipping the egg whites until foamy. Add the salt, then slowly add the sugar, beating until the mixture is thick and glossy and holds stiff peaks.

Remove the bowl from the mixer and use a spatula to move the whipped whites to one side of the bowl, leaving space to add the cooled chocolate on the other side (the chocolate should be no warmer than body temperature). Gently fold the chocolate partially into the whites. I like the look of streaks throughout the meringue, but you can also fold it in completely.

Using a piping bag with a star tip 1 cm in diameter, pipe your desired shapes onto parchment-lined baking sheets.

Bake for about 15 minutes or until the tops are dry and set, leaving the oven door open slightly during baking. They are done when you are able to pick them up off the baking sheet without breaking them.

Biscuits au Vin Blanc

One of Switzerland's best kept secrets is its excellent wine. Per capita, the Swiss are usually in the top ten of wine consuming nations worldwide, drinking about 40 bottles per person per year, according to the federal office of agriculture. However, they only export around a teensy 1-2% of all the wine they make, preferring to enjoy it themselves, at home.

A generous glug of any fine Swiss white wine (Chasselas, Petite Arvine, Malvoisie) is all you need for these beautifully crisp and buttery stars, and if you cut holes in the middle, you can string them around your favourite bottle and give it as a gift.

INGREDIENTS

makes 60

125 g butter, room temperature
150 g sugar
1 egg yolk
pinch salt
50 ml white wine
250 g flour
1 egg white
sugar for sprinkling

METHOD

Cream together the butter and sugar until pale and fluffy. Beat in the egg yolk and salt, then the white wine.

Sift the flour into the butter mixture and stir until combined.

Form into two discs, wrap and chill in the fridge for about an hour, or until firm.

When you are ready to bake

Preheat oven to 180° C.

Roll out the dough to about 0.5 cm thick. Cut out star shapes with a 4-5 cm cutter, place on parchment-lined baking sheets, then cut out a star-shaped hole in the middle.

Brush with egg white and sprinkle with sugar, then bake for 8-10 minutes, or until the bottoms are slightly golden.

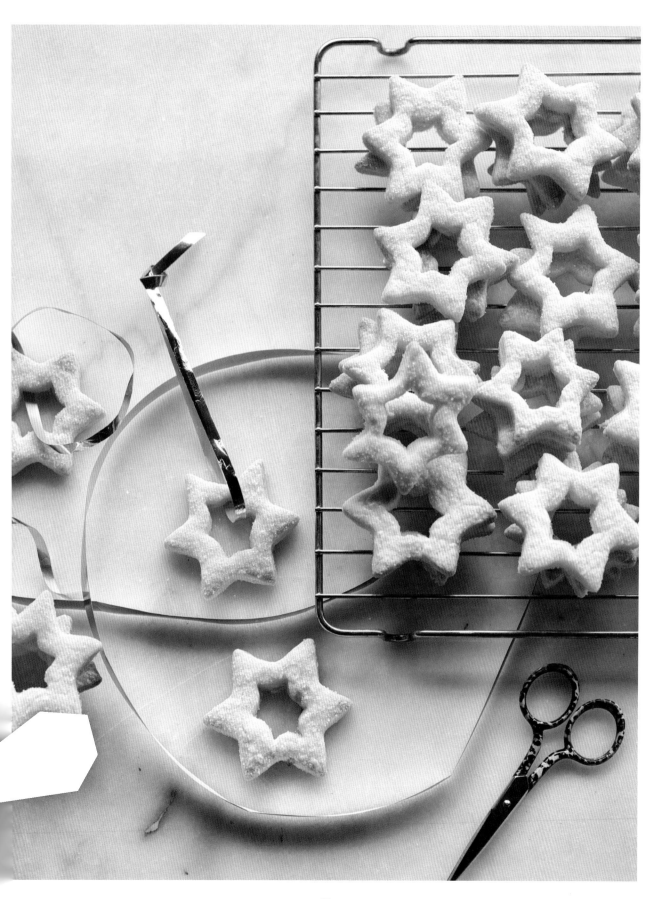

Fuatscha Grassa

Who doesn't love a cookie that's mostly butter?

Fuatscha Grassa are giant, buttery biscuits from the Engadin valley. Local legend regards the giant cookie as a fortune teller. Split one apart on New Year's Day to see how much, or little, luck you will have in the following year, based on how many shards of cookie there are (the more the better).

The ingredients are quite simple, but a century ago they would have been expensive and luxurious – white flour, butter, eggs, and sugar sprinkled right on top. In days past, when white flour was scarce, bakers would have used rye flour, which is what I include in my recipe here.

For me, the appeal (apart from the butter) is the size. It's a substantial cookie, one that might cover your entire plate.

Whether you share or not is up to you.

INGREDIENTS

makes 3

150 g butter, room temperature
70 g sugar
1 egg
1 tsp lemon zest
1/2 tsp salt
170 g light rye flour
sugar for sprinkling

METHOD

Cream together the butter and sugar until pale and fluffy. Beat in the egg, lemon zest, and salt. Sift in the flour and mix until combined.

Form into a disc, wrap and chill in the fridge for about an hour, or until firm.

When you are ready to bake

Preheat oven to 180° C.

Roll out the dough to about 0.5 cm thickness, then using a dessert plate as a template (around 20 cm diameter), cut out large circles with a sharp knife. Place on a parchment-lined baking sheet and sprinkle generously with sugar.

Bake for about 10–12 minutes, or until they are slightly golden around the edges.

Engadinerli

The base of this cookie is made from Fuatscha Grassa dough, the same as is used for Engadine's famous nut tart, Tuorta da Nusch. The tart was originally made by wandering *Zuckerbäcker*, young bakers who fled poverty and military service in Graubünden to work throughout the continent. They stuffed their plain sweet dough with ingredients that were available where they worked, and eventually a caramel and walnut stuffed tart made its way back to Switzerland, becoming a firm favourite with locals and tourists alike.

Bakeries in region sell these little Engadinerli, which are like bite-sized versions of the tart.

INGREDIENTS

makes 32

1 recipe Fuatscha Grassa dough
(page 63)

Topping
250 g sugar
200 ml whipping cream
2 tbsp honey
1 tsp salt
300 g walnuts, toasted and cooled

METHOD

Preheat oven to 180° C, bottom heat.

Roll out the dough into a large rectangle about 1-1.5 cm thick, place on a parchment-lined baking sheet, and chill in the fridge or freezer while you prepare the topping.

Place the sugar in a pot, then shake so it covers the bottom in an even layer. Cook over high heat until it liquifies, and then turns golden, stirring or swirling a little to keep it cooking evenly. Once it is a light caramel colour, add the cream and remove from the heat (careful, it will sputter and seize up a bit), stirring until incorporated. Then stir in the honey, salt and walnuts. Let cool for about 5 minutes.

Take out your chilled base and carefully spread the warm walnut mixture over top. Bake for about 15 minutes, or until the bottom is golden and the top is bubbling. Let cool and slice into diamonds.

Geduldzeltli

These hard little cookies from Zurich and Appenzell (where they are also known as Hosenknöpfli, though not to be confused with the version from Graubünden on the following page), are made with egg whites, sugar and flour. The *Zeltli* of the name is a dialect word for bonbon, and *Geduld*, the German word for patience, is what you need to eat one – they are so hard that you have to patiently let them dissolve on your tongue.

You can flavour them at will, with any essence you have at hand – orange blossom water, lemon essence, rosewater, vanilla...

INGREDIENTS

makes 100+

2 egg whites (70 g)
80 g sugar
70 g flour
2-3 drops of flavouring (vanilla extract, rosewater, orange blossom water, lemon essence)

METHOD

Using an electric mixer with a whisk attachment, start whipping the egg whites until foamy. Slowly add the sugar, beating until the mixture is thick and glossy. Sift in the flour and fold in gently. Fold in the flavouring.

Using a piping bag with a round tip 1 cm in diameter, pipe button-sized circles close together onto two parchment-lined baking sheets.

Let the cookies sit overnight at room temperature.

When you are ready to bake

Preheat oven to 150° C.

Bake the cookies for about 10 minutes, or until they are completely dry but haven't started to brown.

Hosenknöpfli

'Have you made your Hosenknöpfli yet?'

So ask the citizens of the Graubünden towns of Thusis and Masein during Lent. These buttery cookies, traditionally flavoured with rosewater, are a popular treat around that time of year and have been made in the region for over a century.

If you don't have rosewater, rum is an acceptable alternative according to some. It takes time to form all the little buttons, so plan for a bit of work, or enlist some small hands to roll the cookies. The holes in the buttons are not traditional, but I think they add a certain whimsy.

INGREDIENTS

makes 90

50 g butter, room temperature
150 g icing sugar
1 egg
50 ml rum or rosewater
1/2 tsp salt
250 g flour

METHOD

Preheat oven to 160° C.

Cream together the butter and icing sugar until pale and fluffy. Beat in the egg, rum or rosewater, and salt. Sift in the flour and stir until combined.

Taking a handful of dough at a time, roll into logs that are about 2 cm in diameter. Slice off small pieces and roll these into balls, flattening them and placing them on a parchment-lined baking sheet. Dip a skewer in water and use it to make four holes in the centre of each button.

Bake for about 15 minutes, or until the cookies are still pale on top and slightly golden on the bottom.

Hobelspäne

These whimsical little cookies shaped like wood shavings (that's what *Hobelspäne* means in German) were first mentioned in a notable book that is over four centuries old – Anna Wecker's *Ein Köstlich new Kochbuch* from 1597.

Anna Wecker is one of the first women to produce a German language cookbook, and her blend of practical cooking advice mixed with home remedies made her book popular for centuries.

Wecker's recipe for Hobelspäne is different from later versions of the cookie, as hers were made with almonds and rosewater, and they would roll themselves up from the heat.

These ones are made with egg whites and cream, and need to be rolled around the end of a wooden spoon to get their shape. Besides being perfect for snacking, they make a wonderful garnish for ice cream sundaes.

INGREDIENTS

makes 50

2 egg whites (70 g)
100 g icing sugar
75 ml cream
100 g flour
3-4 drops almond extract/bitter almond flavouring

TIP
Alone, I can only manage a batch of about 6-8 at a time. If you want to mass produce, enlist another pair (or two) of hands.

METHOD

Preheat oven to 200° C.

Whisk together the egg white and icing sugar until foamy. Add the cream and whisk well. Whisk in the flour and almond flavouring.

Using a piping bag and flat tip, pipe 6-8 long strips on a parchment-lined baking sheet (about 1.5-2 cm wide and 10-12 cm long).

Bake for around 6 minutes, or until you can see the edges turning golden.

Remove from the oven and immediately twirl around the end of a wooden spoon to make the curly shape. Work as quickly as possible, as the cookies harden as soon as they cool. Repeat with the rest of the batter.

Pane dei Morti

Pane dei morti, Italian for 'bread of the dead', is a cookie that was traditionally baked throughout Italy and Italian Switzerland to commemorate the departed during the festivals of All Saints and All Souls, on November 1st and 2nd.

In late October and early November some Ticino bakeries still sell Pane dei Morti. For bakeries, it is not only a way to use up leftover biscuits and desserts (which were often incorporated into the dough) but also to give customers a taste of the (similarly spiced) Christmas treats to come. Panettone anyone?

A bit chewy and chock full of fruits and nuts, this version of Pane dei Morti is an ode to Ticino, with lots of chestnuts and Nocino, their beloved walnut liqueur. There are lots of ingredients, but that is part of the charm – simply substitute what you have on hand.

INGREDIENTS

makes 26

200 g flour
200 g ground almonds or hazelnuts
200 g candied or caramelised chestnuts, chopped
100 g raisins
60 g brown or raw sugar
50 g pine nuts
30 g cocoa powder
2 tsp cinnamon
1 tsp salt
1/2 tsp nutmeg
120 ml coffee, hot
30 ml Nocino, grappa or other spirit
2 tbsp honey
1 egg white (35 g)

METHOD

Preheat oven to 180° C.

In a large bowl, whisk together the flour, nuts, raisins, sugar, cocoa powder and spices.

Prepare your hot coffee and whisk in the spirits and honey. Let cool until it is no longer hot to the touch, then whisk in the egg white. Pour the liquid into the dry ingredients and mix gently until it forms a dough.

With wet hands, gather the dough and shape into two loaves. Place on a parchment-lined baking sheet.

Bake for about 15 minutes, or until the top has set completely. Take out of the oven and, once it is cool enough to touch, slice it into even pieces (around 2-3 cm thick). Place back on the baking sheet and bake for an additional 10-15 minutes.

Prussiens

Before trading Switzerland for London in the swinging 60s (and subsequently Canada, where I was born) my mother studied hotel management in Zurich.

When it came time to work in the industry, she did what many young hospitality workers did, and spent her winter in Zermatt and summer in Ascona, in sunny Ticino.

She still talks about her time under the snowy Matterhorn working at the front desk of a hotel. There were the Japanese tourists who left decorative envelopes filled with yen on their pillow when they checked out, and Mr Wolf, the American who paid her handsomely to type for an entire afternoon so that his telegrams got to New York on time.

Late at night, once the guests had finished their merry-making, the hotel would open the ballroom to the staff where they could dance and drink.

She befriended one of the chefs and any time she went into the kitchen he gave her Prussiens, her favourite cookie.

In a big hotel, these simple cookies are probably made with leftovers from other dishes and baked goods (vol-au-vents, croissants), but as long as you have some nice buttery puff pastry, these are an incredibly easy and satisfying cookie to make.

INGREDIENTS

makes 30

300 g puff pastry
50 g sugar
1 tsp cinnamon

TIP
This recipe is easy to eyeball – no matter how much puff pastry you have, you can just spread on an even layer of sugar and cinnamon, roll, slice, and bake.

METHOD

Preheat oven to 220° C.

Roll out a sheet of puff pastry, then sprinkle sugar in an even layer over the surface. Sprinkle cinnamon over top.

Roll the long edges in towards the middle, leaving a little space where they meet.

Using a sharp knife, cut 0.7–1 cm thick slices out of the roll and place on a parchment-lined baking sheet.

Sprinkle the cookies with a bit more sugar.

Bake for about 10-12 minutes, flipping halfway through baking.

Totenbeinli

Totenbeinli, meaning 'bones of the dead' (though more literally translated as 'legs of the dead'), are a crunchy, nut-filled cookie originating in Graubünden. This macabre name comes from the fact that they were once commonly served at wakes, and that they should be about as hard and crunchy as the aforementioned bones.

Today they are made year-round throughout the country, and under much more neutral names like Nussstängeli, 'nut sticks', in German, and croquants in French, describing their crunchiness.

INGREDIENTS

makes 34

150 g whole almonds or hazelnuts, toasted
120 g ground almonds or hazelnuts, toasted
100 g butter, room temperature
200g sugar
2 eggs
1/2 tsp salt
180 g flour
1 tsp baking powder
1 tsp cinnamon

METHOD

Once the whole nuts are toasted, set aside a handful to keep whole, and very roughly chop the rest. You will have three kinds of nuts to add: ground, roughly chopped, and whole.

Cream together the butter and sugar until pale and fluffy. Beat in the eggs and salt.

In a separate bowl, sift together the flour, baking powder and cinnamon, then stir into the butter mixture. Fold in the nuts.

Form into a flat loaf (around 30 cm x 15 cm x 1 cm) and place on a parchment-lined baking sheet. Chill in the fridge for about an hour or freezer for about 15 minutes, until firm.

When you are ready to bake

Preheat oven to 200° C.

Bake for about 20-25 minutes or until the top has completely set.

Remove from the oven and wait until it is cool enough to handle. Cut into long slices, place back on the baking sheet and bake for an additional 6-8 minutes or until they are just starting to brown around the edges.

Vanillebrezeln

Enjoyed throughout the German-speaking realm, you'll often find these sweet, vanilla, glazed pretzels on Christmas cookie platters. I like them year round, and I've opted for a pretty pastel glaze to cover the tender, buttery cookie inside.

With so much butter, these cookies can be a bit finicky to get right (though they pretty much always taste great). Although there are rolled versions and cut-out versions, I find it easiest to pipe these cookies. It may take a minute to get the hang of it, but ultimately the results are worth it.

Extra chilling just before baking helps these cookies hold their shape, and the colourful icing helps hide any small inconsistencies.

INGREDIENTS

makes 24

200 g butter, room temperature
80 g icing sugar
1 egg
1 tsp vanilla paste or extract
1/2 tsp salt
250 g flour

Glaze
200 g icing sugar
around 4 tbsp milk
food colouring

METHOD

Preheat oven to 180° C.

Cream together the butter and sugar until pale and fluffy. Beat in the egg, vanilla and salt.

Sift the flour into the butter mixture and mix until combined.

Using a piping bag with a round tip about 1 cm in diameter, pipe 24 pretzels.

Chill in the fridge for about an hour or freezer for about 15 minutes, until firm.

Bake for about 8 minutes, or until the bottoms are golden.

Glaze

Whisk together the milk and icing sugar until you get a thick liquid.

Split the mixture into different bowls and add different colours of food colouring. Depending on the kind of food colouring you use (paste, liquid), you might have to add a little more milk or icing sugar to get the right consistency.

Dip the cookies while they're still a little warm, then place on a cooling rack and let dry.

Zimtpitten

A buttery base, spread with whipped egg whites and topped with toasted almonds, this traybake from Graubünden is extremely delicious. A classic Christmas bake in the canton, I think these deserve to be seen on the table year round.

INGREDIENTS

makes 32

Base
150 g flour
150 g sugar
200 g ground almonds
2 tsp cinnamon
1/2 tsp salt
150 g butter, cold
2 egg yolks

Topping
2 egg whites
30 g sugar
slivered almonds
pearl sugar

METHOD

Preheat oven to 180° C.

Whisk together the flour, sugar, almonds, cinnamon and salt. Rub in the cold butter until you get crumbs. Add the yolks and mix to form a dough.

Directly on a parchment-lined baking sheet, roll out the dough into a large rectangle, about 1-1.5 cm thick. Chill in the fridge or freezer while you prepare the topping.

Topping

Using an electric mixer with a whisk attachment, start whipping the egg whites until foamy. Slowly add the sugar, beating until the mixture is thick and glossy.

Take out the chilled base and spread the egg white mixture on top. Sprinkle with slivered almonds and pearl sugar.

Bake for about 15 minutes in the bottom half of the oven, or until the almonds on top are nicely browned and the bottom is golden.

Let cool, then slice into squares or diamonds.

Züri Härzli

These jam-filled hearts from Zurich are also known as Züri Nüssli and piped into clamshell shapes. Buttery and chocolate-dipped, they are a filled version of a spritz cookie, the delicate treats often served in Germany at Christmas time.

Keeping the dough cool is essential for keeping the nice piped shape of the cookie. You can fill them with any jam of your choosing.

INGREDIENTS

makes 12

200 g butter, room temperature
80 g icing sugar
2 egg yolks (30 g)
pinch of salt
250 g flour

Assembly
150 g jam
150 g dark chocolate, melted

METHOD

Cream together the butter and sugar until pale and fluffy. Beat in the yolks and salt.

Sift in the flour and stir until combined.

Using a piping bag with a star tip 1 cm in diameter, pipe 24 hearts. Pipe two lines about 6 cm each in a 'V' shape, then wet your fingers and press the tails together to make a heart shape.

Chill in the fridge for about an hour or freezer for about 15 minutes, until firm.

When you are ready to bake

Preheat the oven to 180° C.

Bake the cookies for about 8–10 minutes, or until they are set and the bottoms are golden. Let cool completely.

Assembly

Sandwich about a tablespoon of jam between two cookies. Dip one side into melted chocolate

Grandmother's Cookies

'Baking with toddlers is not always the bonding moment I had hoped for,' a friend recently wrote to me.

Agreed.

Sometimes their deft little hands surprise you by removing all the seeds from a pumpkin, or managing to roll a bit of dough, but in my house it is mostly just me regulating the attempted ingestion of ingredients, mostly raw.

'You have to cook that first!' I cry as she tries to chomp potatoes or eat a teaspoon of flour.

Thinking I was clever, I let her bite into a raw onion, but she just grinned and continued eating it like an apple.

'Peel it at least!'

Sometimes you just need the infinite patience of grandparents, who turn a blind eye to the wanton dough consumption and bake happily with their pint-sized kin.

I have three grandmother-inspired recipes – one from my daughter's grandmother, my mother-in-law, Grosi Josy, who loves making big, chocolate and oat Brösmelimonster; one from my husband's grandmother, Marie, who made a very different kind of chocolate oat cookie, Haferflockenguetzli, with lemon icing; and inspired by my own Bernese grandmother, Rosa, the Mandelbär, an almond cookie in the shape of a bear.

Brösmelimonster

In German, Cookie Monster's name describes his finished state rather than his desire – Krümelmonster, 'crumb monster'. That's the name of these cookies in the 1997 cookbook *Das Gästebuch*, put out by the cooperative of Swiss milk producers. I've altered the recipe slightly, scaling up for a monster-sized batch, adding some monster-related decoration, and giving them the Swiss dialect name for crumbs, *Brösmeli* (which is all you will see after your family finds out you've made a batch).

INGREDIENTS

makes 45

375 g butter, room temperature
300 g sugar
3 eggs
2 tsp vanilla paste or extract
1 tsp salt
150 g dark chocolate, melted
400 g flour
30 g cocoa powder
1 tsp baking powder
150 g oats (fine)

To decorate
pine nuts
royal icing (see page 136)

METHOD

Cream together the butter and sugar until pale and fluffy. Beat in the egg, vanilla, and salt. Stir in the melted chocolate (it should be warm but not hot).

In a separate bowl, sift together the flour, cocoa powder, and baking powder. Stir in the oats. Add to the butter mixture and stir until fully combined.

Using a scoop or a tablespoon, place 4 cm balls onto a parchment-lined baking sheet. Chill in the fridge for about 30 min or freezer for about 10 minutes, until firm (but not frozen).

When you are ready to bake

Preheat oven to 180° C.

Press cookies flat, dipping your hands in cold water when they get sticky. Press the pine nuts into the cookies so they look like monster teeth.

Bake for about 8 minutes or until the tops are set.

Let cool completely, then ice on monster eyes using royal icing.

Grosi's Haferflockenguetzli

These hearty, crunchy cookies are a classic from my husband Sam's childhood. Although I occasionally opt not to ice them, in Sam's mind this is a cardinal sin and the slight tang of lemon glaze is essential.

INGREDIENTS

makes 32

75 g butter, room temperature
125 g sugar
1/2 tsp salt
150 g flour
1 tbsp cocoa powder
1 tsp baking powder
150 g oats
75 ml milk

Glaze
2 tsp lemon juice
50 g icing sugar

METHOD

Cream together the butter and sugar until pale and fluffy. Beat in the salt.

In a separate bowl, sift together the flour, cocoa powder, and baking powder. Stir in the oats.

Stir half of the flour mixture into the butter mixture, stir in the milk, then stir in the rest of the flour mixture.

Form into a disc, wrap, and chill in the fridge for at least an hour or until firm.

When you are ready to bake

Preheat oven to 180° C.

Roll out the dough to about 0.5 cm thick. Cut out cookies with 4-5 cm cutters in desired shape and place on a parchment-lined baking sheet.

Bake for about 10-12 min.

To make the glaze, whisk together the icing sugar with lemon juice a teaspoon at a time until you get a runny glaze. Brush onto the cooled cookies.

Mandelbären

While writing this book, my Aunt Vreni sent me some of my Grandmother's old recipes. Her Kleine Mandelbretzeln (little almond pretzels) were dipped in a mix of almonds and sugar before baking. I eschewed the fiddly task of rolling pretzels and cut out bears instead in a nod to Bern, my grandmother's home canton.

INGREDIENTS

makes 28 bears

200 g flour
120 g ground almonds, toasted and cooled
120 g sugar
1 tsp salt
100 g butter, cold
2 eggs

Glaze
1 egg, lightly whisked
pearl sugar
almonds (slivered, chopped, etc.)

METHOD

In a large bowl, whisk together the flour, almonds, sugar and salt.

Add the butter and rub into the mixture with your hands until you get small crumbs. Add the egg and mix to form a dough.

Form into a disc, wrap and chill in the fridge for about an hour, or until firm.

When you are ready to bake

Preheat oven to 180° C.

Roll out the dough to 0.7 cm thick, cut out bears (or other shapes), and place on a parchment-lined baking sheet.

Brush with egg and sprinkle with pearl sugar and almonds.

Bake for about 10–12 minutes, or until the cookies are nicely golden.

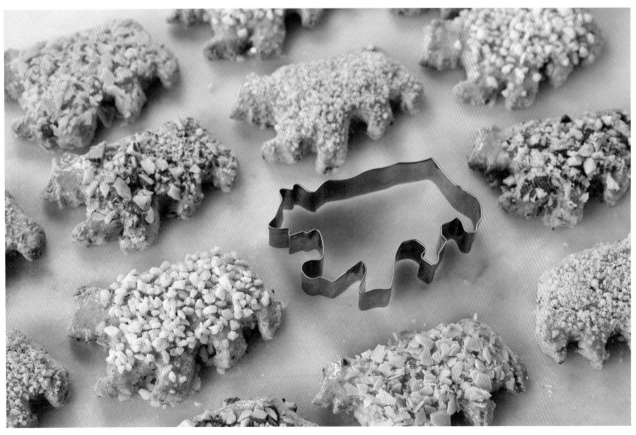

Guetzliteig

This versatile dough (I'm calling it Guetzliteig) can be used as a base for many different cookies, including the classic jam filled Pfaffenhüetli and Vogelnestli (see the following pages), plus chocolate, vanilla or marbled cut-outs. You can split it in half and use it for two different recipes, and it freezes wonderfully as well.

There are many Swiss themes you can cut into the dough, from crosses to edelweiss. And, as cookies are often used to commemorate events or people, I would like to salute my favourite Swiss residents, the cows. These long-lashed, long-tongued beauties deserve, at the very least, a cookie in their honour.

INGREDIENTS

yield depends on the size of the cookie cutters

Vanilla Dough
170 g butter, room temperature
150 g sugar
1 egg
1 tsp vanilla paste or extract
1 tsp salt
300 g flour

METHOD

Cream together the butter and sugar until pale and fluffy. Beat in the egg, vanilla, and salt. Sift in the flour and stir until combined.

Form into a disc, wrap and chill in the fridge for an hour, or until firm.

When you are ready to bake

Preheat oven to 180° C.

Roll out the dough to between 0.5–0.7 cm thick. Cut out the cookies in your desired shapes and place on a parchment-lined baking sheet.

Bake for about 10–12 minutes.

Let cool, then decorate with royal icing (page 136).

For cocoa dough: substitute 270 g flour and 30 g cocoa powder.

For marbled dough: follow the first step of the recipe above, adding all the ingredients except the flour (and cocoa powder). Spilt the butter mixture into two bowls (around 190 g in each bowl), and in one, sift in 150 g flour, and in the other sift in 135 g flour and 15 g cocoa powder. To marble, very lightly knead the two doughs together.

Pfaffenhüetli

Pfaffenhüetli ('priest's hats') are named after its shape, which recalls a biretta, a three- or four-cornered hat worn by the clergy. Today, these pyramids are often filled with nuts and sold in bakeries and supermarkets.

However, taking a look back into old cookbooks these cookies were called by many slightly varying names (which all mean 'little priest's hats') and filled primarily with jam. Susannah Müller's 1860 cookbook describes her Pfaffenkäppchen as four-cornered and filled with *beliebige Fruchtmarmelade* (arbitrary fruit jam), while Rosa Graf from 1947 uses thick, *saurer Konfitüre* (sour jam). Sophie Wermuth from Basel (1908, *Die junge Köchin*) puts nuts in her Pfaffenkäppli dough and fills them with *dicklicher Konfitüre* (thickish jam). The textbook from Zurich's domestic school first published in the 1930s suggests apricot, raspberry or red currant jam for their Pfaffenhütchen.

Taking their advice, I have eschewed the typical nut filling which can often be dry and flavourless, preferring different sorts of jam or jelly.

INGREDIENTS

makes 32

1 recipe Guetzliteig (page 93)

Assembly
about 150 g jam
1 egg, lightly whisked

METHOD

Preheat oven to 180° C.

Roll out the dough to 0.5 cm thick and use 7 cm cutters to cut out rounds. Place about a teaspoon of filling in the middle of each round.

Using your fingers, lift up the edges to make three points. Be sure to press the points together really well or they will come unstuck when baking and the filling will leak out.

Brush the outside with egg, then bake for about 10–12 minutes, or until golden.

Vogelnestli

Glimmering in Swiss bakery windows are the weighty Vogelnestli (little bird's nests), with a buttery base and nutty meringue border filled with jam. Sort of like a mix between Linzer and Spitzbuben, these cookies are a perennial favourite.

INGREDIENTS

makes 24

1 recipe Guetzliteig (page 92)

Topping
4 egg whites (140 g)
120 g sugar
360 g ground nuts
2 tsp cinnamon
1 tsp salt
200 g jam

METHOD

Preheat oven to 200° C.

Roll out dough to 0.5 cm thick. Cut out rounds 8 cm in diameter and place on a parchment-lined baking sheet. Chill in the fridge or freezer while you prepare the topping.

Topping

Using an electric mixer with a whisk attachment, start whipping the egg whites until foamy. Slowly add the sugar, beating until the mixture is thick and glossy. Fold in the nuts, cinnamon, and salt.

Assembly

Take out the chilled cookie bases. Using a piping bag with a star tip 1 cm in diameter, pipe the topping around the edge of each cookie. Fill the centre with jam.

Bake for about 15 minutes or until the nutty meringue has browned slightly and the bottoms are golden.

Swiss cookies: reimagined

Here I have a selection of cookies developed using some of my favourite, particularly Swiss ingredients:

Absinthe: once a banned substance in Switzerland (and many other countries) for its much-exaggerated psychoactive properties, this green spirit originally comes from the Val de Travers, in the canton of Neuchâtel. It's made from a blend of anise, fennel, wormwood, and other botanicals, and its strong liquorice flavour lends itself well to baking.

Birnenhonig: a syrup made of pears and also known as Birnendicksaft, Birnel (a slightly lighter version), or, in the French speaking part of Switzerland, vin cuit or raisinée. Fruit (not just pears, but sometimes apples or grapes too) is boiled down until it becomes dark, sweet, sticky, and molassesy. Traditionally, it was made in big copper pots over open fires.

Magenträs: Canton Glarus' pink sandalwood sugar is sold in little packets with an iconic picture of a grinning boy on the front. The *Magen* in the name is the German word for stomach, and Magenträs was purported to help soothe upset tummies. It works well for baking, and it adds a lovely pink gleam when sprinkled over buttered bread.

Nocino: a liqueur made from green walnuts, available throughout Europe, but particularly enjoyed in Ticino. It's made by soaking the nuts in spirits (usually grappa) until the liquid turns black and bitter, then sugar and spices are added to make a complex, nutty, bittersweet drink.

Ovomaltine: this mix-in-milk powder, was created in Bern in 1904 as a nutritional supplement for children of the day. Eventually it became one of Switzerland's most popular brands, at home and afar. If you're in the English-speaking realm, you'll see it sold as Ovaltine, so named because of a mistake on the British patent in 1909, but in Switzerland you'll likely hear its even shorter nickname, Ovo.

Absinthe Sablés

During the late 1800s absinthe became the drink of choice for the bohemians in Paris, and the likes of Baudelaire, Toulouse-Lautrec, Zola, and Gauguin imbibed the spirit, known as the 'green fairy'.

Generally, I like drinking absinthe alone with a swirl of cold water while pretending to be a French bohemian, but its strong anise taste lends itself well to cooking and baking, especially in these buttery cookies.

INGREDIENTS

makes 24

150 g butter, room temperature
80 g icing sugar
1 egg yolk
1 tbsp absinthe
1/2 tsp salt
200 g flour
1/2 tsp baking powder

Glaze
200 g icing sugar
1 egg white
1 tbsp absinthe
green food colouring

METHOD

Cream together the butter and sugar until pale and fluffy. Beat in the yolk, absinthe, and salt.

In a separate bowl, sift together the flour and baking powder, then stir into the butter mixture until combined. Roll the dough into two logs about 5 cm in diameter.

Chill in the fridge for about an hour, or until firm.

When you are ready to bake

Preheat oven to 180° C.

Cut the logs into 1 cm thick rounds and place on a parchment-lined baking sheet. Bake for about 10 minutes or until the bottoms are golden.

To glaze

Sift the icing sugar. Whisk the egg white until foamy, then slowly whisk in the icing sugar and the absinthe. Place two thirds in a shallow dish for dipping the cookies, reserving the rest for the decoration.

Once the cookies are cool enough to touch, but still warm, dip their bottoms in the glaze (this way you get a nice flat surface for decorating), then place them glaze-side up on a cooling rack. Let cool completely, then colour the remaining glaze and decorate.

Birchermüesli Guetzli

Apples are the main ingredient in Dr. Maximilian Oskar Bircher-Benner's healthy 'mush', his Birchermüesli. Combined with oats, condensed milk, lemon juice, and nuts, Birchermüesli embodied his ideas about the importance of raw food in the treatment of disease. He experimented with raw food diets in his famous sanatorium on the Zürichberg and eschewed the idea of animal proteins, preferring vegetarianism.

Chock full of apples, oats and nuts, these vegan cookies are a nod to Dr Bircher and his famous Müesli.

INGREDIENTS

makes 16

200 g whole wheat flour
100 g oats
1 tbsp ground flaxseed
1 tsp baking powder
1 tsp cinnamon
1 tsp salt
200 g apple, grated
100 g peanut oil (or other neutral tasting oil)
80 g Birnenhonig, light molasses, or treacle
50 g raisins
50 g walnuts, toasted and chopped
cinnamon sugar to sprinkle

METHOD

Preheat oven to 180° C.

Stir together the flour, oats, flaxseed, baking powder, cinnamon, and salt.

In a large measuring cup, mix together the grated apple, oil, Birnenhonig, raisins and nuts. Gently stir into the flour mixture until combined.

This is a sticky batter, so wet your hands or the spoons with cold water before dropping ping-pong shaped balls onto a parchment-lined baking sheet. Sprinkle with cinnamon sugar.

Bake for about 12–15 minutes, or until they are lightly golden.

TIP

Raisins and walnuts are only a suggestion – you can use any kind of nut and dried fruit – pecan and cranberry, almond and apricot, or hazelnut and prune are also good options.

Birnenhonig Cookies

These cookies are a play on the soft, chewy ginger or molasses cookies I loved to eat growing up in Canada, only instead of molasses adding the flavour and chew, this recipe employs Birnenhonig, a syrup made from pears (more on page 99).

I like using Birnel, a lighter version of the syrup, but if you prefer a more powerfully fruity taste go with a darker one.

INGREDIENTS

makes 36

180 g butter, room temperature
80 g sugar
1 egg yolk (15 g)
150 g Birnenhonig (Birnel preferred)
1 tsp salt
320 g flour
1 tsp baking soda
1 tbsp Lebkuchen spice mix

sugar for rolling

TIP

If it is very warm in your kitchen and the batter feels really soft, you can chill the dough in the fridge or freezer after you have formed the cookies, before baking. Don't have Lebkuchen spice mix? You can make your own – recipe on page 136.

METHOD

Preheat oven to 180° C.

Cream together the butter and sugar until pale and fluffy. Beat in the yolk and then the Birnenhonig and salt.

In a separate bowl, sift together the flour, baking soda, and spice mix. Stir into the butter mixture until combined.

Using a scoop or your hands, form ping-pong sized balls and roll them in sugar. Place on a parchment-lined baking sheet, using your hand to press them down flat.

Bake one sheet at a time for about 8–10 minutes, or until set on the sides and just barely set in the middle.

Magenträs
Snickerdoodles

Magenträs is a pretty pink spiced sugar made in canton Glarus and flavoured with sandalwood (more on page 99). The sugar lends not only a distinct taste, but also a rosy sparkle to classic, cakey Snickerdoodles.

INGREDIENTS

makes 22

120 g butter, room temperature
120 g sugar
1 egg
1/2 tsp salt
200 g flour
1/2 tsp baking powder
1 packet Magenträs powder (30 g)

METHOD

Preheat oven to 180° C.

Cream together the butter and sugar until pale and fluffy. Beat in the egg and salt.

Sift together the flour, baking powder, and salt, then stir into the butter mixture.

Form ping pong-sized balls, roll in Magenträs and place on a parchment-lined baking sheet, pressing them down flat.

Bake for about 10–12 min or until the tops have set and the bottoms are golden.

Nocino Biscotti

Just like in Italy, you'll find biscotti in Ticino, ready to be dipped into something warm, like coffee, or boozy, like Vin Santo. I like to add a hint of booze to my biscotti dough and dip them in my favourite Ticinese liqueur, Nocino.

INGREDIENTS

makes 20

120 g sugar
50 g melted butter
2 eggs
1 egg yolk
1 tbsp Nocino
zest from one orange
250 g flour
2 tsp baking powder
1 tsp salt
100 g walnuts, toasted and cooled
1 egg white, whisked
sugar for sprinkling

METHOD

Preheat oven to 180° C.

Whisk together the sugar, melted butter, eggs and yolk, Nocino and orange zest.

In a separate bowl, sift together the flour, baking powder, and salt. Stir into the sugar mixture until combined. Roughly chop the walnuts and fold in.

Using wet hands, form the dough into a rectangle on a parchment-lined baking sheet.

Brush the loaves with whisked egg white, sprinkle with sugar, then bake for about 20 minutes, or until the tops are starting to brown slightly.

Remove from oven, let cool slightly, then cut into slices on the diagonal. Place these back on the baking sheets and bake for an additional 10 minutes, or until they are dry and browning at the edges.

For best results, dip in Nocino before eating.

Ovomaltine Sandies

Ovomaltine adds some extra sandiness to this double chocolate cookie. The highlight is the rim – first brushed with egg white and then rolled in Ovo – which has a delightfully sticky bite. More on Ovo on page 99.

INGREDIENTS

makes 24

200 g butter, room temperature
160 g sugar
220 g flour
15 g Ovomaltine
15 g cocoa powder
1 tsp baking soda
1 tsp salt
150 g chocolate, chopped

1 egg white (35 g)
Ovomaltine powder

METHOD

Cream together the butter and sugar until pale and fluffy.

Sift together the flour, Ovomaltine, cocoa powder, baking soda and salt. Stir into the butter mixture. Stir in the chopped chocolate.

Form into two logs about 5 cm in diameter, wrap in plastic, and chill in the fridge for about an hour, or until firm.

When you are ready to bake

Preheat oven to 180° C.

Brush the whole log with egg white and roll in Ovomaltine powder.

Cut the logs into 1 cm thick rounds and place on a parchment-lined baking sheet. If they fall apart during cutting, just press them back together.

Bake for about 8-10 minutes or until the tops have just barely set.

Tuiles Bäckerei Wegmüller

Mixing traditional and modern

The villagers in the small town of Gerzensee in the Berner Oberland could always tell the Christmas season had begun simply by opening their windows. They knew by the smell of spiced Lebkuchen from the ovens of Bäckerei Wegmüller, wafting through the town as the months turned cold.

The heart of that warm bakery is where Björn Wegmüller grew up, already the fifth generation of bakers. His great, great grandfather started the business in 1896 as a traditional Swiss bakery with bread and pastries – and, of course, Lebkuchen at Christmas time.

Although the location has now changed and the Wegmüller bakery sits on a little corner in Langnau im Emmental, the Lebkuchen recipe has remained the same.

Lebkuchen, meringues, and above all Tuiles make up Bäckerei Wegmüller's product range today. It was Björn's parents who added Tuiles to the mix, crunchy rolled biscuits, sweet or savoury, and secured a contract with Globus to distribute them all over the country. This eventually led to the bakery shop closing to focus on Tuile production.

That is until 2016, when Björn and his wife Sabrina found a new home for the historic bakery. Toting decades-old bakery paraphernalia from the original location – handwritten recipe books, wooden moulds with Bernese bears and his grandfather's initials, an old Felchlin chocolate tempering machine, a textbook from 1946 exclusively about Lebkuchen – they opened their new storefront.

Sabrina's eye for design and Björn's bakery know-how are a winning combination, and together they manage to preserve the bakery's past while making it feel thoroughly modern.

When I visited Björn and Sabrina, they were eagerly awaiting a new addition to their family (one that could potentially become the next generation of Wegmüller bakers), so I asked them about their own earliest cookie memories. Originally from Davos in canton Graubünden, Sabrina remembers baking the local specialty Totenbeinli with her grandmother, who baked according to feeling – a little of this, a handful of that – and whose cookies always came out perfectly. (You can also try your hand at this specialty – my recipe for these nutty cookies on page 76.) Of course, Björn remembers the bakery kitchen, sneaking Mailänderli and Lebkuchen while they were cooling on trays. A memory that their own child can look forward to one day soon.

Tip

Love, patience, and a dash of courage.
Take your time, but don't be afraid to try new things.

Swiss Christmas Cookies

In December, when days are cold and there's little sunlight, Swiss families often gather together to bake cookies. It's an important feature of Advent, the run up to Christmas, with some families making over a dozen different varieties. The most beloved Christmas recipes are dusted off, a schedule is made, recipes are double-checked and maybe a new one is added to the rotation.

There are calculations, like how many eggs do I need if I use yolks for the Mailänderli and whites for the Brunsli? Butter inevitably goes on sale, and so do ground nuts and parchment paper, which means perusing supermarket flyers and writing detailed shopping lists. Some mills even offer 5 kg bags of *Guetzlimehl,* flour that's fine and perfect for cookie making.

Ingredients are prepared – chilled, toasted, warmed, ground – and tools and tins are brought forth, as well as promises from family members to help with certain parts of the baking day(s).

Each variety of cookie is carefully stacked in its own tin, and when guests come to call, or you are invited to someone's house, a plate is arranged with the many cookies on display, often according to preference. When my mother-in-law prepares a plate for our family, she puts out extra raisin cookies for my husband and extra Spitzbuben for my daughter. If my mother comes for tea before Christmas, I leave off the Zimtstern and double up on the Anischräbeli, sending her home with a plate as well.

I remember my childhood cookie baking; finally being allowed to cut out the Mailänderli, sneakily taste-testing the dough ('you'll get worms in your tummy!' my mother would cry, echoing the words of my Bernese grandmother), then arranging the cookies on a serving plate, one for the plate, one for me.

The big four: Switzerland's favourite Christmas cookies

No festive cookie tin in the German or French part of the country would be complete without the big four, perennial holiday favourites: Mailänderli/Milanese, Brunsli/Bruns de Bâle, Zimtsterne/Étoiles à la cannelle, and Spitzbuben/Miroirs.

Every family has their own way of making the cookies, with some favouring long drying times, and others adding kirsch at every chance. In our family the dough was always rolled quite thick, and the cookies were tall and robust. Some prefer a store bought dough, while others make a dozen or more different varieties from scratch. But however you make your cookies, they probably include some mix of the big four.

I make mine according to recipes from my mother and grandmother, who liked their Mailänderli towering and buttery, their Brunsli bursting with chocolate, their Zimtstern icing as white as possible, and their Spitzbuben filled with red currant jam. I prefer mine with raspberry, but otherwise I follow their advice on these four Christmas classics.

Basler Brunsli / Bruns de Bâle

Typically known as Basler Brunsli, these chocolatey cookies are forever associated with the city of Basel and were initially baked there, not only at Christmas, but also for weddings and other special occasions.

There is debate over which nuts to use, whether almonds, hazelnuts, or even walnuts. Some recipes call for grated or melted chocolate, while others depend on cocoa (and some, like this one, use both). Finally, some recipes suggest the cookies should be baked low in the oven and some forgo baking completely and just leave them out to dry.

INGREDIENTS

makes 60

200 g ground nuts
200 g sugar
100 g dark chocolate, grated
80 g cocoa powder
2 tsp cinnamon
1 tsp salt
3 egg whites (105 g)
2 tsp kirsch

TIP

I normally use ground almonds, but hazelnuts work well too. I have also tried ground walnuts, which are very delicious.

METHOD

Mix together the nuts, sugar, chocolate, cocoa powder, cinnamon, and salt.

Using an electric mixer with a whisk attachment, whip the egg whites until stiff. Fold in the dry ingredients and kirsch.

Form into two discs, wrap, and chill in the fridge for about an hour, or until firm.

When you are ready to bake

Preheat oven to 200° C.

Using sugar, roll out the dough to around 0.7-1 cm thick, then cut out with 4-5 cm cutters and place on a parchment-lined baking sheet.

Bake the cookies for about 8 minutes, or until you can smell them and their tops look dry.

Mailänderli / Milanese

These are the standard Swiss Christmas cookie made by nearly every bakery and every family in the country. Buttery with a hint of lemon, the taste is a nostalgic reminder of childhood and Christmas for Swiss people throughout the world.

In the 19th century, the cookies featured at New Year's parties in Basel where the Baslers called them *Gaatoodemylängli,* from the French *gâteaux de Milan* and served them with their famous mulled wine, Hypokras.

INGREDIENTS

makes 40

Dough

125 g butter, room temperature
125 g sugar
3 egg yolks (45 g)
zest from one lemon
pinch of salt
250 g flour

Glaze

1 egg yolk (15 g)
pinch sugar

TIP

If the dough looks dry once you have mixed in the flour, you can add a little more yolk or a little milk. Using just yolks makes for a beautifully rich and golden dough, but you can swap out the three yolks for one whole egg, if desired.

METHOD

Cream together the butter and sugar until pale and fluffy. Add the egg yolks one at a time, beating well. Beat in the lemon zest and salt. Sift in the flour and mix until combined.

Form the dough into two discs, wrap, and chill in the fridge for about an hour, or until firm.

When you are ready to cut and bake

Preheat oven to 180° C.

Roll out the dough to about 0.7-1 cm thick. Cut out the cookies with 3-4 cm cutters and place on parchment-lined baking sheets.

For best results, chill again in the fridge for about an hour, or the freezer for about 15 minutes.

For the glaze

Whisk together the egg yolk and sugar and brush an even layer on the cookies.

Bake for about 10 minutes, or until the glaze is set and the bottoms are golden.

Spitzbuben / Miroirs

The jewel of the Swiss Christmas cookie tray is surely the Spitzbuben, with its elegant dusting of icing sugar and bright ruby centre. Spitzbuben are a relatively modern cookie in Switzerland, and were likely developed and named in the 20th century. The term *Spitzbub* refers to a mischievous boy, and the cookies may be so named because jammy faces were originally cut into the dough.

This method involves rubbing the butter into the flour, and the final product is tall, buttery and crispy. It does, however, benefit from being kept cold, and it dislikes re-rolling. If you don't have the patience, or you have little helpers who like to play with the dough, I suggest using my Guetzliteig dough (recipe on page 93) which is much more forgiving.

INGREDIENTS

makes 26

250 g flour
80 g sugar
pinch of salt
150 g butter, cold
2 egg yolks (30 g)

Assembly
120 g jam
icing sugar

METHOD

Whisk together the flour, sugar, and salt. Add the cold butter in pieces and rub into the flour mixture with your fingers until it is sandy. Add the yolks and mix to form a dough. If the dough seems dry, or won't gather up, just add a little cold milk or water, a tsp at a time.

Form into two discs, wrap, and chill in the fridge for about an hour.

When you are ready to cut and bake

Preheat oven to 180° C.

Roll out dough to be 0.5 cm thick and cut out cookies 5 cm in diameter, trying not to work the dough too much when you re-roll.

Place on a parchment-lined baking sheet, then cut an additional hole in half the cookies to make the tops.

Bake for 10–12 minutes, or until just golden.

Assembly

Dust icing sugar over the tops. Sandwich about a teaspoon of jam between a top and bottom cookie, pressing together until the jam peeks out the hole.

Zimtsterne / Étoiles à la cannelle

Zimtsterne (cinnamon stars), also popular in Germany, have been around in some form or other for centuries. In the Middle Ages they were a luxury – cinnamon being particularly treasured and sufficiently expensive.

There are plenty of recipes to be found, though the most arduous recipe I've seen comes from 1892 via Rosina Gschwind, a Bernese educator, women's rights activist, cookbook author, and founder of two domestic management schools, who suggests beating the egg whites and sugar by hand for an entire hour. Luckily today a good whirr with an electric mixer does the trick in mere minutes.

INGREDIENTS

makes 60

3 egg whites (105 g)
250 g icing sugar, sifted
350 g ground almonds
2 tbsp cinnamon
1 tsp ground cloves
1 tsp kirsch

METHOD

Using an electric mixer with a whisk attachment, start whipping the egg whites until foamy. Slowly add the sifted icing sugar, beating until the mixture is thick and glossy.

Remove about 150 ml of the egg white mixture, cover with plastic wrap and leave in the fridge to use later as icing.

Mix together the ground almonds, cinnamon, and cloves. Add the remaining egg white mixture and kirsch, and stir until you have formed a dough. The dough should not be crumbly, and if it looks dry at all, add back a teaspoon or two of the reserved icing.

Using icing sugar, roll out to about 0.7-1 cm thick, then cut out with a 4-5 cm star-shaped cookie cutter and place on a parchment-lined baking sheet. Dip the cutters in icing sugar to prevent sticking.

When you are ready to bake

Preheat oven to 200° C. One at a time, put the baking sheets on the bottom rack of the oven and bake for about 5-7 minutes or just until they get just a bit of colour at the edges.

While the cookies are still warm, dip in the reserved icing. Alternatively, you can ice the cookies before baking – they set nicely, but it's harder to keep them perfectly white.

The Anise Paradise

Cookie moulds for every occasion

From the outside, besides a small sign on the mailbox, there is nothing to indicate that Linus Feller and Petra Mösli live in an anise paradise (anise cookies that is, also known as Änisbrötli or Springerle, whose delicate designs are made with intricate moulds).

However, visit the narrow room at the back of their house and it's a different story – over a thousand different models, stacked on shelves from floor to ceiling.

'Go to the end and look left,' Petra says.

Behind the shelves is a stone wall, part of Nidergösgen's Schlosskirche, the church which towers above their cosy home.

Every mould is numbered, and both Linus and Petra know them by heart. From this organized cavern their moulds are packaged and sent all over the world or, for many years, the pair toured of autumn and Christmas markets throughout Switzerland, Germany and France, selling their wares on location.

Their market stand was legendary (it even won the prize for most beautiful stand at the Basel Christmas market in 2017), and customers visit year after year with success stories, thank-yous, and complaints that they still can't get their Füsschen quite right. This would always turn Petra and Linus into cookie detectives – how long did you let them rest? Did you use parchment paper? Did you weigh the eggs? Was there a draught? Anything to help the public bake their best.

Besides the models, they sell Änisbrötli from their own recipe (no kirsch), their own anise spice mix, and even marzipan, another baked good that takes well to moulding.

Models have fascinated Linus for over three decades and he has been collecting them for about as long. Over the years he has gained the trust of curators and collectors alike, who have allowed him to restore and replicate their beloved models and pass the designs on to further generations.

And that itself is not an easy task. Old forms show their age over time and it's up to Linus to painstakingly form these one-of-a-kind pieces in silicone, making sure none of the historic wear and tear is transferred to the new mould. Once the models are repaired, a *Mutterstück* can be created (the copy from which subsequent models are made), and the original returned to its owner. Then a silicon form is made, and from that the commercial moulds, with a special kind of high-quality resin that is waterproof and works like a dream.

Linus and Petra collaborate with professional wood carvers (notably the renowned Neff family in Appenzell) to design new models. The wood carvers draw the suggested scenes and then carve them into pear wood, making 10-20 motifs each year. They rely on the public to help them decide which new moulds are made each year, often choosing quite modern designs along with the traditional to make sure the art form stays relevant in future and appeals to their international markets, especially customers in the US.

Upon publication of this book, the exact number of different moulds for sale in the anise paradise was 1104, though this number grows every year.

Basel loves Änisbrötli

But not everyone does...

Historically, southern German cities like Stuttgart and Ulm were hubs of Springerle production and consumption but, according to Linus (of the aforementioned anise paradise), the Basel region is the real *Weltmeister* (world champion). Änisbrötli are baked there throughout the year and celebrate everything from baptisms to weddings. The Baslers love their cookies, and to them an Änisbrötli isn't an Änisbrötli without a drop of kirsch.

Moulded cookies are nothing new, as they have been made since Roman times and are known to depict all manner of things – religious scenes, decorative motifs, everyday work. However, it was in Germany, more precisely Stuttgart, where these anise moulded cookies, also known as Springerle, originated.

They were initially popular in the north of Switzerland, especially in Basel, where something similar has been made since the 17th century. During this time, Änisbrötli were a poor man's version of a very luxurious treat, Marzipan. Remove the expensive ground nuts and you had 'farmer's' or 'common' marzipan, a beautiful, decorative cookie that the masses could afford.

Today, the pale, elegant, anise flavoured Änisbrötli (made with moulds) and Anischräbeli (spiky, curved) are a popular, if polarizing, Christmas cookie.

For some, it's the liquorice flavour that doesn't agree with them, and for others, it's the threat of a tooth-breaking bite that makes them shy away from these pretty treats. There isn't a lot to be done for anise-haters, but there are plenty of ways to prevent a bland, brittle, or dry biscuit.

When done right, these cookies are pale on top, slightly chewy in the middle, and have the customary *Füsschen*, feet, on the bottom. When the cookies bake, the pale, white crust rises up leaving a layer, the *Füsschen*, visible underneath. Along with resting for at least 24 hours, the bottom of the cookie needs to and stay moist and protected from the air, to allow it to rise in the oven – which means greasing the baking sheet directly with butter, rather than using flour or parchment paper. If the dough is not sufficiently mixed and rested, the cookies will not rise.

Änisbrötli or Chräbeli

These anise flavoured cookies can be pressed into intricate wooden forms, or made into simple spiky logs. A tip from the Anise Paradise, purveyors of wooden forms and master Brötli bakers? Weigh your eggs.

INGREDIENTS

makes 45 Chräbeli
(Brötli will depend on the size of the forms)

butter for greasing
2 eggs (110 g)
250 g icing sugar
250 g flour
shot of kirsch
1 tbsp anise seeds, lightly toasted

METHOD

Grease two baking sheets with butter.

Using a stand mixer with a paddle attachment, whip together the eggs and icing sugar. Keep whipping for about ten minutes, or until you get a thick, pale paste. Sift in the flour and fold in. Fold in the kirsch and anise seeds.

Let the dough rest for about ten minutes, then it is ready to use.

For Brötli (forms)
Using flour, roll out the dough to about 1 cm thick. Dust with more flour and press with floured wooden forms to create designs on the surface. With a cutter or knife, cut out individual pieces and gently brush off excess flour. Place on the greased baking sheets.

For Chräbeli
Roll the dough into logs about 2 cm in diameter and cut into 6 cm tubes. Make 3 slightly diagonal cuts in one side of the dough and curve slightly. Place on the greased baking sheets.

Let dry for at least 24 and up to 48 hours. Don't disturb your cookies while they are resting – find a dry spot that isn't draughty.

When you are ready to bake

Preheat oven to 150° C (do not use convection).

Keeping the oven door slightly ajar, bake the cookies for about 20 minutes, or until they are fully dried out and have (hopefully) risen on their *Füsschen*.

Lebkuchen

Brought by Samichlaus (the Swiss St Nick) on the 6th of December, this version of gingerbread is seen all over Switzerland during the holiday season.

Fragrant with spices and sometimes stuffed with marzipan, these cookies and breads can be elaborate and ornate, easily serving as decoration, or be unfussy and simply delicious to eat.

My version contains more butter than most, and is meant for cut-out cookies. To keep it soft in the middle, be sure not to overbake, taking them out of the oven just as the bottoms start to brown. If you prefer a breadier Lebkuchen, you can follow the recipe for Biberli dough on page 30 – whether you stuff it or not, is up to you.

INGREDIENTS

makes 16 large cookies

150 g butter, room temperature
100 g sugar
2 eggs, room temperature
200 g honey
450 g flour
1 tsp baking powder
1 tsp baking soda
1 tbsp Lebkuchen spice mix
1/2 tsp salt

To decorate
Royal icing (page 136)

TIP
Don't have Lebkuchen spice mix? You can make your own – recipe on page 136.

METHOD

Cream together the butter and sugar until pale and fluffy. Beat in the eggs, then the honey.

Sift together the flour, baking powder, baking soda, spice and salt. Add to the butter mixture and stir until combined.

Form into three discs, wrap and refrigerate for at least an hour, or until firm.

When you are ready to bake

Preheat oven to 180° C.

Roll out dough to about 0.7–1 cm thick, cut out the cookies with 10–12 cm cutters, and place on a parchment-lined baking sheet.

Bake for about 11 minutes, or until the bottoms are starting to brown.

Let cool completely and decorate with royal icing.

Macaroons

A perennial Christmas favourite, these easy and infinitely variable cookies require no resting or chilling, and are a great way to use up leftover egg whites. Made all over the country, the macaroons from the picturesque village of Sent in the lower Engadin surely have the most evocative name. They are called *puglinas*, a Romansch word that means 'chicken poop'.

You can vary their contents as you see fit. Some families make them bite-sized, and put a whole nut on top, but I like mine around the size of a ping pong ball and dipped in chocolate.

INGREDIENTS

each recipe makes 16

Almond
2 egg whites (70 g)
60 g sugar
200 g ground almonds
1 tsp bitter almond/almond extract

Coconut
2 egg whites (70 g)
60 g sugar
2 tsp rum
170 g unsweetened coconut

Pistachio
2 egg whites (70 g)
60 g sugar
200 g salted pistachios, shelled and ground in a food processor or small grinder

Cocoa Hazelnut
2 egg whites (70 g)
60 g sugar
180 g ground hazelnuts
20 g cocoa powder
zest of half an orange

METHOD

Preheat oven to 180° C.

Using an electric mixer with a whisk attachment, start whipping the egg whites until foamy. Slowly add the sugar, beating until the mixture is thick and glossy.

Gently stir in the nuts and flavouring. Form into balls and place on a parchment-lined baking sheet. If the batter is too sticky, wet your hands with cold water.

Bake for about 8 minutes or until the bottoms are golden.

If desired, dip in or drizzle with chocolate.

TIP
Whipping the egg whites will make for a light and crispy cookie, however you can make a simplified version that leaves out this step (and is great for kids to help with), just lightly whisk the egg white with the sugar, then stir in the nuts and flavouring.

Vanillegipfeli

Vanillegipfeli are tender, buttery, croissant-shaped cookies, dredged in vanilla icing sugar. Originally from Vienna, and more commonly known as Vanillekipferl, these cookies are popular in many parts of Europe.

They are notoriously fickle, bursting with butter, and prone to breaking during the forming of the crescent. Work the dough too much and they lose their tenderness, but too little and the dough falls apart in your hands. Don't chill enough and they spread wildly on your baking sheet, though they'll still taste delicious.

INGREDIENTS

makes 36

200 g butter, room temperature
100 g icing sugar
1 tsp vanilla paste or extract
220 g flour
120 g ground almonds
1/2 tsp salt

For dredging
100 g icing sugar
the seeds of half a vanilla bean,
or 1 package of vanilla sugar

METHOD

Cream together the butter and sugar until pale and fluffy. Beat in the vanilla.

Whisk together the flour, ground almonds and salt, then add this to the butter mixture. Mix until it resembles large crumbs.

Gently press the crumbs together into three rolls, wrap, and refrigerate for about an hour, or until firm.

When you are ready to form

Taking one cylinder at a time from the fridge, slice each into about 12 rounds, form into little sausages, then bend into crescents. Place on a parchment-lined baking sheet.

These cookies are prone to spreading, so for best results chill in the fridge for about an hour or freezer for about 15 minutes.

When you are ready to bake

Preheat oven to 180° C.

Bake for about 10–12 minutes, or until their bottoms are golden, but they are still pale on top.

While they are baking, mix the icing sugar and vanilla in a bowl.

Once the cookies are out of the oven, let them rest for a minute or two, then dredge them in the vanilla icing sugar.

Appendix

Marzipan
150 g blanched, ground almonds
1 tsp cinnamon
80 g icing sugar
1 egg white (35 g)
a few drops bitter almond or almond extract

Whisk together the almonds and cinnamon, then sift in the icing sugar. Add the egg white and extract, then mix until you get a thick paste.

TIP
If you don't have blanched, ground almonds, you can use regular ground almonds, or grind slivered almonds with the icing sugar in a food processor until fine.
Can be wrapped airtight and kept in the fridge for up to a week.

Lebkuchengewürz
If you can't purchase a good Lebkuchen spice mix, it's easy enough to make your own at home:

15 g ground ginger
15 g ground cinnamon
15 g ground aniseed
10 g ground coriander
5 g ground cardamom
5 g ground nutmeg
5 g ground cloves

Mix together and store in an airtight container.

Royal Icing
1 egg white (35 g)
about 200 g icing sugar, sifted

Using a mixer with a whisk attachment, start beating the egg white. Once it is foamy, begin adding icing sugar, a couple of tablespoons at a time. When it reaches your desired thickness, stop adding the icing sugar.

If you want to make the icing thicker, add a bit more icing sugar. If you want to make the icing thinner add a drop of water (about 1/2 tsp at a time).

Use a wet towel or paper towel to cover the icing in the bowl so it doesn't dry out.

I typically fill parchment paper piping cones with royal icing to do decorative work. If you need help making one, there are lots of great tutorial videos online.

Help!
Something's amiss!

A gentle troubleshooting guide for finicky cookie doughs

The dough is too dry

Before chilling:
Resist the urge to knead it together, as this can create a tough cookie, and instead try adding a little milk to the dough until you can bring it together.

After chilling:
If it's still crumbly, let it warm up a little longer and very gently work the dough, pressing crumbs back in, until it is pliable. Roll it out between pieces of parchment or plastic, rather than adding more flour.

The dough is too sticky and I can't roll it out

Make sure the dough has been properly chilled.

If you have a flour-based dough, use flour to help you roll it out (you can always brush off excess flour with a pastry brush), or try rolling between sheets of parchment or plastic.

If it is a nut-based dough that doesn't contain flour (Brunsli, Zimtstern) then it is best to roll it out using granulated or icing sugar. You can dip your cookie cutters in water when they start to get sticky. If it is impossible, you can add some extra ground nuts to the batter.

How do I know when the cookies are baked?

Start checking on the cookies as soon as you start to smell them. For most cookies, I err on the side of taking them out when they are slightly underdone, as the residual heat from the baking sheet will continue to bake them. They will firm up as they cool.

To help you know when to take the cookies out of the oven, I've tried to give visual hints in the recipe – tops set, bottoms golden – as oven temperatures and baking times can vary from oven to oven.

Resources and Further Reading

While researching this book, I was lucky to have recipes from my own family and the family of my husband to consult, as well as a large collection of old Swiss cookbooks and textbooks.

There are numerous Swiss educators who published cookbooks and, in some cases, founded domestic schools, and their recipes provide insight into the development of Swiss cookies over the decades. The writing of Susannah Müller (*Das Fleissige Hausmütterchen* 1860), Rosina Gschwind (*550 Rezepte von Frau Pfarrer Gschwind*, 1892), Sophie Wermuth (*Die junge Köchin*, 1908), and Rosa Graf (*Goldene Kochfibel*, 1947) were particularly helpful, as was the recent book by Sabine Bolliger *Köchinnen und ihre Rezepte*, 2014 from Werd und Weber Verlag.

Also helpful and inspiring were cookbooks from two of the Grand Dames of Swiss food writing, namely Marianne Kaltenbach's *Aus Schweizer Küchen* (1977, Hallwag Verlag) and Elisabeth Fülscher's *Kochbuch* (1960, Selbstverlag Elisabeth Fülscher). The elegant Christmas cookie book *Eigelb und Puderzucker* by Karin Messerli (2009, Werd Verlag) is another classic of the theme.

The great historian Albert Spycher wrote the seminal work on Basler Leckerli, *Leckerli aus Basel*, published by the Buchverlag Basler Zeitung in 1991.

Interested in the history of wooden cookie forms? Check out Linus Feller's 1998 book *Änismodel*, available at springerle.com. Also available there is Christa Fischer's beautiful book *Stolze Reiter, schöne Damen* from Jan Thorbecke Verlag, 2012.

Want to do more with your Bretzeli press? Ursula Kambly's 2007 book *Das Kambly-Bretzeli* from Stämpfli Verlag has 24 sweet and savoury recipes.

Bewährte Kochrezepte aus Graubünden (Tried and Tested recipes from Graubünden) is a little spiral bound treasury of some of Graubünden's most beloved recipes (including cookies) and can be ordered online through the Gemeinnützigen Frauenverein Chur, sgf-chur.ch.

If you want to learn more about Swiss culinary history in general, your first port of call is the *Kulinarisches Erbe der Schweiz / Patrimoine culinaire suisse / Patrimonio culinario svizzero / Patrimoni culinar svizzer*, patrimoineculinaire.ch.

Merci Viel Mal

To all the proofreaders, proof-bakers, proof-eaters thank you!

Thanks to the team at Bergli and Helvetiq. It's always a delight to work with you, Richard. Thank you Kali for your artistic eye. And a big thanks to Kim, you always make everything into such a polished whole.

It was a thrill to visit some of Switzerland's most beloved cookie producers, many thanks for opening up your bakery doors and letting me have a peek inside.

Urusla Kambly, for the generosity of your time, and your beautiful books. To Carlo Magnano, for telling me the fascinating history of the Suter Tirggel Factory.

It was a delight to be able to visit one of Switzerland's oldest companies – thank you Andreas for sharing the story of Jakob's Basler Leckerly. And I'm so lucky that Tuiles Bäckerei Wegmüller is just around the corner, thanks Sabrina and Björn for telling me your stories. Thanks also to Beat and Evelyn at the Haldemann Mill for being so flexible and generous with your time.

And a huge thanks to Linus and Petra at the Anise Paradise - what a thrill to visit you and see your incredible wooden forms. Thank you for taking the time to tell me their history and your history too. And thank you for the beautiful books.

Thank you to Cornelia Zogg from the Gemeinnützigen Frauenverein Chur for helping me source the Hosenknöpfli recipes. And many thanks to my Aunt Vreni for passing on my grandmother's recipes and to the Bucheli family for trusting me with Marie's recipes. Thanks Johanna, for sharing the secret to your family's Bricelets.

I was delighted to be able to call in the expertise of an actual archivist during my research—thanks Florian! And to my excellent team of proofreaders, thank you Mary, Stuart, Jackie, Allana and Allie. And my proofeaters, Jessie, Tilly and Dan, thanks for letting me ply you with cookies.

I wouldn't have been able to write and photograph this book without the help and support of my mother Rosemarie, my parents-in-law Josy and Robi, and my sister-in-law Franziska, who helped with everything from childcare, taste-testing, providing props for the photographs, showing me secret family recipes, and being reluctant models. Thank you.

My favourite cookie tasters, Stella, who grabs them hot off the trays, and our neighbour Walter, who has a kind word for every cookie in this book, merci viel mal.

And the biggest thanks of all goes to my husband Sam for his invaluable help with translation, photography, and cookie tasting. I'll never forget the lemon icing again.

Where to buy

Swiss Cookies

• Basler Leckerli: Jakob's Basler Leckerly, baslerleckerly.ch (ships internationally); as well as many bakeries in Basel.

• Zürcher Leckerli: Sprüngli, spruengli.ch (ships internationally)

• Berner Haselnusslebkuchen: Olo Marzipan, olomarzipan.ch; Tuiles Bäckerei Wegmüller, tuiles-baeckerei.ch (both ship within Switzerland); as well as many bakeries in Bern.

• Bärli-Biber: almost any Kiosk, supermarket, gas station, bakery, bar or cafe in the country

• Kambly Bretzeli: Kambly, kambly.com (ships internationally); as well as most Swiss supermarkets

• Surseer Honiggans: Bäckerei Konditorei Stocker, Sursee.

• Tirggel: Suter Tirggel, tirggel.ch; St Jakob's Stiftung, st-jakob.ch (both ship within Switzerland).

• Tuiles: Tuiles Bäckerei Wegmüller, tuiles-baeckerei.ch (ships in Switzerland); as well as Globus.

• Willisauer Ringli: Café Amrein in Willisau, willisauerringli.ch (ships in Switzerland); as well as most Swiss supermarkets.

Ingredients and Tools

• Birnenhonig/Birnel: Winterhilfe, winterhilfe.ch; this non-profit organiztion has been selling Birnel in Switzerland since 1952 and the proceeds go to families in need. You can also find it in many Swiss supermarkets (near the jam) and Landi.

• Magenträs Trietolt: Glarussel, glarussell.ch; and shops in the Glarus region.

• Teighölzli: these wooden or plastic stick for rolling dough can be found in the bakeware section of most Swiss supermarkets and department stores.

• Wooden cookie moulds: order these from the Anise Paradise springerle.com (ships internationally).

Index